AGAINST ALL ODDS

The Story of a World Champion who
Turned his Trauma into Triumph.

Tyree Washington

DEDICATION PAGE

I would like to thank my grandmother, Lee Ethel Williams, my mother, Mattie Williams, my coach Blackman Ihem, and my wife, Monica Washington, for helping to make my dreams become a reality.

TESTIMONIALS

"Tyree's story can teach us all how human spirit and willpower can burn bright enough to transcend circumstances through embracing what is difficult and greeting it head on with unflinching bravery."-Amy Acuff, 5-Time U.S. Olympian in track and field.

"Tyree Washington was not supposed to make it based on statistics of kids who grew up in the type of environment that he did even with sports as an outlet. Not only did he battle the odds to get into school to further his education himself, he was able to take his life experiences and use them as positive motivation to create a better life for himself and propel his athletic career to unattainable heights. Tyree is a warrior, and I will go to battle with him any day." - Patrick J. Johnson, Super Bowl XXXV champion and West Valley Eagles Track Club teammate.

"In life, we can succeed at whatever we set our minds to achieving. Tyree's book will point you in the right direction." - Lawrence Rawson, Emmy Award winning track and field commentator.

"Tyree Washington is a preeminent example of out of your misery comes your ministry. A true inspiration to all those that have fallen down and seek inspiration to get back up." - Mark Crear PhD, two-time Olympian.

"Tyree's story is truly about overcoming the odds. He had every aspect of life stacked against him as a young adult. This story is one that will inspire young, old, and professionals alike, especially the youth." - Blackman Ihem, Tyree's personal track coach

"We knew we had a special one. Tyree had it all. He was fast, he was tough, good-looking, and most importantly, he had possessed that inner spirit. As a young football recruit coming out of La Sierra High School, he didn't know it, but as a recruiter, I did. I knew he could be great. I know what it looks like. However, I couldn't foresee the circumstances which would galvanize and shape Tyree into the world champion that he is today. Ty's story is a road map of perseverance, faith, and finish. This is a must read for anyone and everyone facing adversity and hardship but holding strong to vision and hope. You are not alone—and Ty wants you to know that you can do it!

Don Pellum, UCLA football, inside linebackers' coach

ACKNOWLEDGMENTS

First, I would like to thank God for giving me my athletic talent. I want to thank all the family, friends, and fans who gave me continued encouragement throughout my personal life and professional athletic career. There are so many people I want to give credit to. If I don't mention you, please forgive me, and just know you were a vital piece of the puzzle to help me become the man I am today. I believe every successful person has a village of positive people who have contributed to their success.

I'd like to thank my mom, Mattie Lee Williams, and my grandmother, Lee Ethel Williams, for loving me unconditionally and for supporting me through good times and bad. I am grateful for my sister, Rosalyn Washington, who was always honest with me—showing me right from wrong when I was a young boy. I want to thank Annette Gomez, Edward and Barbara Rivas, Sherri Compton, Sandy Grizzle, Cathy Dugger, William and Joanetta Taylor, Coach Phil Julick, Coach Bill, Coach Bo, Coach Peterson, Chris Reid, Ruben and Nadine Gilbert, Debbie and Dan Passalacqua, Hank Moore, Cami and Dwight Berry, Raymond Aguirre, Rick Garza, Charles Graves, Gil Lake, Ken Blumenthal, and Mike Powell—all for being surrogate moms and dads to me while I was on my life journey—working to make my dreams become a reality.

To Coach Blackman Ihem, you were a godsend to me when I was in a dark place in life and didn't know if I would ever be able to pursue my goal of becoming a collegiate or professional athlete. You broke me down and built me back up to become, not only a great athlete, but also a man of God who helps people in need; regardless of their race, financial status, culture, or living situation. Your words of wisdom and unconditional love for me have been imprinted on my heart and will be with me until the end of time. I also want to thank all my track and field agents; Roger Lipkis, Kimberly Holland, Renaldo Nehemiah, Pete Peterson, Greg Foster, and Caroline Feith, and NFL agents Dr. Harold Daniels and JJ Flournoy, who spent many late hours negotiating deals to help me and my family. Many thanks to my childhood friends Mike Acedo, Nian Taylor, Robert Grizzle, Sean and Leslie Compton, Jeremy Udstrand, Jason Lazono, Benny and Nano Sanchez, Ameel Cody, Jason Ramberg, Jermaine Hawkins, Pete Garza, Young Lee, Gabe Rivas, DeAndre Watson, Matt and Bryan Lewis, Kevin Nielsen, Jerome Garcia, Patrick Johnson, and Bryan Howard for supporting me when I was just an average boy daydreaming about being on the big stage.

TABLE OF CONTENTS

FOREWORD

Athens, 1997. It was the world championships, and the first time I had ever met Tyree Washington. Surrounded by athletes at the peak of their game, we shared the track for the semi-final of the 400m, and his easy smile and swagger made him stand out from the pack. He seemed ten feet tall, and I will never forget watching him punch the air in exuberant celebration as he flew across the finish line to victory. Despite being the new kid on the block, Tyree exuded confidence, and it was matched by his talent. He was truly the embodiment of boundless potential blooming into reality.

Every athlete present had followed their own unique path to the world championships, but we were bound together by our mutual un-conditional love for the sport. Having pushed our bodies to the limit every day, committing our entire lives to our craft, picking up injuries and overcoming setbacks, we had finally been brought together for the opportunity of a lifetime, representing our countries and hoping to bring home a medal. Tyree won the bronze medal in the 400m final behind the great Michael Johnson, and we shared the rostrum for the 4x400m relay, with the USA just triumphing over us for the gold. To me, this medal represented everything I had ever worked for. It was a culmination of my lifelong dream, countless hours at the track, the sacrifices I had made, and my most paralysing struggles. The euphoria was incomparable, and I felt like I was floating with joy—a feeling I know that Tyree shared. The air was electric, and the moment was life changing.

Thirteen years later, this golden moment was to be forever scarred by scandal. Like two sides of the same coin, both Tyree and I were blown away by its undeniable impact in opposite ways. However, whilst our suffering seemed to be converse, our fates became intertwined by the struggles we shared. To have ascended to the pinnacle of achievement and have basked in the glory of a dream achieved, Tyree was stripped of his honours and left tarnished, perhaps ineradicably so, by the actions of his teammate. Despite retrospectively being awarded the gold medal, I did not feel like a winner. I became haunted by what could have been, having been deprived of the opportunities that the gold medal would have brought. Both of us were left with a shattered image of what we had previously understood our careers and our lives, to be.

The whole affair was steeped in suffering. Antonio Pettigrew committed suicide, leaving behind his wife and children in the wake of the scandal. This sent shockwaves through the community, and I can't even begin to articulate the crippling pain this must have caused his family. For both Tyree and myself, we were left to reconstruct our perceptions of ourselves and our futures. To have worked all your life for a dream, see that dream turn into your reality at the expense of your blood, sweat, and tears, only to have it torn apart by something out of your control, is powerfully destructive. But, it can also be powerfully transformative.

Tyree's story paints a portrait of human suffering, and the way it can transform your life. From the highest peaks of achievement to the deepest pits of struggle, this story chronicles the journey from the top to the bottom and back to the top again. The story of travelling between suffering and success is common to us all, and the inevitability of human suffering can often be paralysingly scary. His story will show you that in times of hardship, you have the strength to overcome this fear and suffering, find consolation in the courage required to take action, and transform yourself into a stronger and more resilient version of yourself.

Whilst the impact of the scandal left a permanent impression on my character, the pain it caused forced me to make a crucial choice; remain embittered and forever haunted by fantasies of what could have been or accept that I will never truly escape its legacy, using it as an opportunity to grow and make my peace with my history. The choice was not an easy one, and suffering, in all its infinite forms, can often feel inescapable and unbearable. To alleviate this burden, one must turn to the stories of others, draw strength from their ability to conquer hardship and emerge transformed. I know that I have found courage in Tyree's story, and I know that you will too.

Jamie Baulch, Olympic silver medalist and 3x world champion

PREFACE

We all have a story to tell, and I want to share mine with you. Imagine we're in my living room sitting on the sofa. I'm taking you on a journey and giving you a vivid picture of my life. Let me start by saying, I've spent my entire life going against the current and being the underdog. I've had many highs in my life that have lifted me up, but the low times have broken me down to the point where I didn't know if I would ever get back up.

I've always struggled with asthma, and it almost took my life many times. If you've ever been punched in the stomach or ever tried breathing through a straw, you will quickly realize that every breath you take is vital to your existence. I compare asthma to life, because in life, you will encounter lots of adversity dealing with your finances, career, marriage, and family that will take your breath away. This can cripple you for a short time, but once you recover, you will be back on your feet, taking the necessary steps to get to your destination. I've realized that life is not fair, and life may put you in a situation you don't want to be in, but if you take advantage of your talent and use it to the fullest, you can turn your tragedy into triumph.

I was born in Riverside, California, and raised by a single mother and my grandmother. Growing up, I was surrounded by violence and poverty every day. My only ticket out of my war zone was sports, and it helped to mold me into a man that loves people and family. My goal is to share my life experiences in the hope that it will give you inspiration, motivation, and hope. I know many people in the world have gone through what I've gone through—or they are going through it right now, and they need a pick-me-up. My prayer is that my book will touch your life, rejuvenate your faith, and whatever problems you're going through in life, you will learn to overcome them. My book is called, *Against all Odds*, because I know there are billions of people world-wide who have a desire to do something very special in the world, but circumstances have prevented or slowed them down from reaching their goal. When you read through the pages of this book, you will see how I turned my trauma into triumph. I have also included Tyree's Top Ten Takeaways for Success that will give you guidance, motivation, and encouragement to help you succeed at whatever you pursue in life.

I hope you enjoy reading my story and allow it to penetrate your heart and soul. Please, let it help you strive for greatness not perfection. We can never be perfect, but we can surely become better every day. To me, sharing my story is about planting positive words in people and then watching those people blossom into phenomenal human beings.

Chapter 1

Born Into the Struggle

The scene was electric. Everywhere I looked, fans were flying flags from their countries. A crowd of 100,000 people screamed with intense excitement as each race concluded. The frenetic tension was palpable. It was the 2003 World Track and Field Championships in Saint Denis, France, and I knew I owned the 400 meters. Success was mine. I could feel it. I had the best training of my life in the fall of 2002. Leading up to Saint Denis, I was undefeated on the European circuit, executing each race to perfection. My soul, though, was in turmoil because of a family tragedy that nearly set me off course.

Just months earlier, I learned that my sister got sentenced to twenty-five years to life for killing her fourteen-month-old daughter because she claimed my niece had mental problems; so she tortured, bound her hands, and starved her to death. For her murder, my sister was sentenced to life in prison. I was haunted by my last visit with my niece Anjulette. I realized something was not right in the home, but what made me feel reassured everything would be ok was when I found out from my sister's boyfriend's family that Child Protective Services did a wellness check on Anjulette, and they stated everything was OK. My world nearly spiraled out of control. The only place I could find freedom from this unspeakable tragedy was on the track, or on the road, or at the beach. Running cleared my mind of all the pain and hurt. I was like a tiger that didn't eat for months. And so, when I ran, I ran with vengeance for Anjulette and to deal with my own guilt. In my mind, running made everything right. The only thing that was going to stop me from winning a world championship was God Himself. And, God knew all that I'd overcome to get to this place.

My mother, Mattie, was twenty-five years old when she got pregnant with me. She was scared and extremely fearful to tell my grandmother, Lee Ethel, so she hid her pregnancy for nine months. My grandmother would ask my mother, "Are you in a family way?" (meaning are you pregnant), and my mom would reply, "Ain't nothing wrong with me." For months, my mother would wear oversized clothes to avoid showing any signs of pregnancy.

On the evening of August 27, 1976, my mother was at a party with family and friends when she went into labor. All hell broke loose when my aunt Betty noticed water running down my mother's leg and yelled at my mom, "Mattie, you got water running down your leg!" My mother, being in denial, replied to my aunt, "That's nothing!" My aunt said, "Mattie, you're pregnant!" When word got back to my grandmother that my mom was pregnant, my grandmother said, "As sure as I am cooking these greens, I knew Mattie was with child. She was carrying him up high—that's a boy."

My aunt Betty and her friend Helen called the paramedics while my mother stood still like a "deer in headlights". While waiting for the paramedics, Aunt Betty and her friend Helen were outside in the parking lot arguing back and forth about what my name would be. My aunt said, "Mattie, what do you want to name your baby?" My mom replied, "I don't know—you and Helen name it." Aunt Betty wanted to name me Shannon, and Helen wanted to name me Tyree. So, the feud went on until finally the paramedics intervened and told my aunt and Helen, "Why don't you give him both names and please shut up!" My aunt and Helen decided to do it the diplomatic way by flipping a coin to see who got to name me first. To Helen's surprise, she won the coin toss. Tyree became my first name, and Shannon became my middle name. I asked my aunt why she and Helen gave me those names. She said, "Tyree and Shannon were two soldiers who fought in the Civil War. Tyree was a Confederate soldier who fought with the Gray Coats, and Shannon was a Yankee who fought with the Blue Coats."

My mother gave birth to me at Riverside General Hospital, in California, on August 28, 1976, at 6:17am. I weighed in at six pounds, fourteen ounces, and was nineteen inches long. My family seemed to be in awe that I didn't have any health problems, considering my mother hid her pregnancy for nine months and didn't receive any prenatal care. The following day, I went to my new home in Casa Blanca, CA. Little did I know, the months ahead were going to be very difficult. Four months after my mother delivered me, she battled psychological issues, which overwhelmed her to the point that it was hard for her to take care of me. I spent many days hungry, sick, and visiting the emergency room. The nurses and doctors diagnosed me with "failure to thrive," and when I was four months old, I was hospitalized for a week. I lost a lot of weight—so much weight that Social Services got involved to place me in another home. However, my grandmother and aunt stepped in to help take care of me. I was literally fighting for my life, and I wasn't even a year old yet.

When I was about a year old, I started to develop breathing problems which turned into full-blown asthma. My hospital visits were like clockwork throughout the years. I was hospitalized for at least three days and three nights—one week here, one week there. When I was released to return home, another asthma attack awaited me. Soon, I was back at the hospital repeating the cycle again. With all the chaos going on in my young life, my father chose to be absent, even though he lived just minutes away, right in Casa Blanca. As I got older, stronger, and more resilient, my mother and family seemed to be shocked that I was beating the odds.

I desperately wanted my father to comfort me during my time of struggle, but he was never there for me. I often cried until I had no more tears, and my mother would do her best to console me. I knew that I had a father, and it just broke my heart that he didn't want to have anything to do with me. My mother, my two sisters, and I left Casa Blanca at the end of 1979 because the crime was so bad that a man got killed right in our front yard. We moved to the Jurupa area of Riverside, California, into a two-bedroom apartment to be in a safer environment and closer to my grandmother. My mother couldn't work, as she was on disability, so my two sisters and I were put on welfare. At the time, my mother thought living in the Jurupa area was a good idea, but this neighborhood was also flooded with crime. I remember a time when my mother found out that a lady in our neighborhood had put her hands on me and my two sisters. She went outside in the middle of the street and fought the lady as if she were a professional boxer. My mother didn't get arrested that day because the fight was broken up very quickly. If the cops *did* come and start asking questions, it was a code in my neighborhood that whatever happened in our neighborhood stayed in our neighborhood.

I went to Rustic Lane Elementary School in Riverside, and Ms. Terry was my kindergarten teacher. When I first saw her, my eyes lit up like a Christmas tree. She looked like an angel that was sent by God to personally take care of me. I remember that her scent was sweet as cherry pie, and her voice was soft as a baby's bottom. I was a scrawny, little kid who looked deathly ill, but she comforted me like I was her own child and made sure I was happy every day. Being with Ms. Terry at school was a relief from being in my drug and gang-infested neighborhood. Soldiers, in the military, go to boot camp to prepare for war. Well, the streets were *my* boot camp. Even at a young age, you were taught to hide your emotions and never show weakness—or you might end up dead.

I remember a time when I was playing football on the blacktop at Rustic Lane with my friend, and he yelled, "Tyree, go deep!" So, I started running like a bat out of hell, looking up at the sky and stalking the football as if it were my prey. Suddenly, I heard voices yelling at me, "Tyree, look, out!" I quickly turned my head and immediately connected with a pole, splitting my nose wide open. I lay spread-eagled on the blacktop, completely knocked out. When I woke up, I asked my mom what happened, and she told me I hit a pole. I remember going to the hospital, but after that everything seemed blank. From that day on, I realized that if I can hit a pole and get back up, I shouldn't fear anybody in my neighborhood.

Eventually, things got so bad in our neighborhood, with all the drugs, gangs, and violence, my mom decided we should all go live with my grandmother and uncle in a less violent part of Riverside. My grandmother, aka, "Big Momma," and my uncle had a four-bedroom house and a dog named Toby. He had a white coat and looked scraggly, even anorexic at times. I felt relieved we were finally among family and living in a decent neighborhood. My uncle seemed very authoritative to me, but maybe I felt that way because I never had a father figure to look up to. Although I was a very young boy at the time, my uncle gave me responsibilities. I was responsible for picking up dog poop in the back yard and helping clean up the front yard. My uncle taught me algebraic equations, while he was studying to become an electrician. My mom never interfered with what my uncle wanted to do with me because she feared him, though at times, they would get into disagreements about how my sisters and I should be raised. One time, my mother was bathing me and my two sisters together in the bathtub when my uncle walked by and told my mom that boys shouldn't be bathing with little girls. I really didn't think bathing with my sisters was a bad thing until my uncle told my mom that it wasn't appropriate.

Big Momma was the glue that kept the family together. She made sure the house was clean, clothes were washed and pressed, and that every Sunday all the family was together. I loved my grandmother very much! She wouldn't allow too many people in her kitchen while she was cooking, but she allowed me. I would stand on a chair and watch her paint a masterpiece while making all the Southern dishes. She wanted to make sure, since I was the only boy, I learned how to cook at a young age. I would watch her cook gumbo, macaroni and cheese, and cake—and she never used a measuring cup for any of it. I was in awe of how she maneuvered around the kitchen like a Nascar stock car driver. I would ask her, "Grandmother! How do you know how much seasoning to put in the food?" My grandmother would reply, "I just can feel it baby!" She was right because when all the food was cooked, it tasted phenomenal.

My grandmother was a very superstitious woman and believed in Hoodoo. (Hoodoo is a form of magic that comes from Africa and is mostly practiced in the Southern states in America.) You couldn't sweep when the sun went down, and if you swept someone's feet with the broom, you'd better spit on the broom or something bad would happen to you. You couldn't whistle in the house because that was considered bad luck. My grandmother kept her room cold, and she kept two broomsticks shaped like a cross under her bed. I asked her what the broomsticks were for, and she said they were there to ward off witches. I was freaked out! I once told my grandmother I saw the rocking chair in the living room rock back and forth with nobody in it and that the cabinets would sometimes open and shut by themselves. She would nonchalantly tell me, "Oh, that's one of our family members, so don't pay no mind to that." I couldn't help but love my grandmother, but I was seriously scared of her beliefs and the house we lived in!

Big Momma's love, though, always made you feel secure enough to go for your dreams. She provided the foundation that assured you whatever you did in life, you would be okay. Being raised in struggle always made me want to work hard, so I could have a more comfortable life someday. Racing the kids in the neighborhood and beating them, helped me discover early on, I could always get ahead of someone else when I needed to.

My asthma didn't get any better living with my grandmother. I continued to have asthma attacks, and having the ambulance come pick me up at my grandmother's house was a regular occurrence. I was always sick with a cold or flu, but that didn't keep me from playing outside with my sisters, cousins, and friends. My mother, grandmother, aunt, and uncle didn't look at asthma as a handicap. They treated me like any other child in our family. I would get sick a lot more than any child or adult in our family, thus I had to work two or three times as hard to be like a normal kid.

I was always a curious kid and was open to new adventures. A few friends in my neighborhood built a treehouse in a rundown area—about a block away from my grandmother's house. The treehouse was pretty raggedy. The wood was decaying, and my friends used two-by-fours for steps and nailed them to the tree. Once, in this makeshift treehouse, I noticed *Hustler* magazines all over the floor. I was always curious about what a woman looked like without clothes on, and so *Hustler* helped to fulfill that curiosity. One day, we listened to Madonna's song, *Like a Virgin*, on my buddy's radio while in the treehouse. It was ironic that I was looking at *Hustler* magazine—knowing nothing about sex at the time—and Madonna's song, *Like a Virgin,* was playing on the radio! I spent many days in that tree house with other boys looking at *Hustler* magazines until I moved. If my mom, grandmother, aunt, or uncle knew what I was doing up there, I would have been beaten like there was no tomorrow.

My uncle really loved me and my sisters. There was a dairy about a mile and a half away, and my uncle took me and my sisters there occasionally to get super sundaes. He would put me on his shoulders; my sisters would be glued to his hip, and we would all sing as we walked to the dairy, "I'm going to get a super sundae, I'm going to get a super sundae. I got to have it. I need it. I'm going to get a super sundae." Those were great times with my uncle. At the time, he was the father I never had.

We enjoyed living at grandmother's house—it was a breath of fresh air from the gangs and the violence we were used to. One day, though, my grandmother's house caught on fire due to a faulty pipe, so we all had to move. My grandmother was devastated because she loved her home, and she loved having her own privacy.

Chapter 2

Montgomery Village aka "The Ville"

Most people think you have to go to war to experience mortal violence, but living in Montgomery Village apartments, also known as the Ville, in Riverside, California, we saw it every day. My mother and grandmother moved to the Ville in the early '80s after her house burned down because of an electrical problem in the home, thinking it would be a great place to raise me and my sisters, but they didn't realize living in a poverty-stricken environment was such a dangerous place for us to be. I was a scrawny, little kid who walked around with my inhaler in my pocket, wearing worn out pants with holes in them, and my Payless shoes. I hated the fact my mother couldn't afford name-brand shoes because I would always see the Original Gangsters aka OGs in the Ville rocking nice shoes, jeans, kango hats, and wearing gold chains. I wanted to be like them so badly, but I knew even at that young age, that everything came with a cost.

Being in the Ville was like being in prison. If you wanted to survive, you always had to have your head on a swivel—showing no weakness and never allowing anyone to disrespect you. And, when it was time to fight—you'd better knuckle up! I was never jumped into a gang, but I claimed my allegiance to the Crips. The Ville was a tight-knit community, and everybody knew everybody, but you still needed protection from outside gangs, and people who might try to rob and kill you. I never had a dad, and the OGs I hung around with were like fathers to me. They knew my mom was on disability, and we were on welfare, struggling to make ends meet. They would drop a $20 bill in my pocket to give to my mom, and I would earn a little cash by being a runner and dropping off a dime or nickel bag of weed from time to time.

I remember a time back in California when the OGs would go to the river bottom to smoke weed and shoot guns, and I would be the only little boy there with all these grown men. The river bottom was under a freeway near Van Buren Street, in Riverside, CA. It had a little pond, and I remember seeing two little ducks in the water. One of the OGs asked me, "Hey cuz, you ever shot a gun?" I said I hadn't. He took his hand, reached behind his back, and pulled out a 22 pistol. My adrenaline was pumping, and all I could think of was, "I'm eight years old, and I'm about to bust these bullets all over the river bottom." He told me the gun was loaded but on safety. He stood behind me with his hands overlapping mine, and he helped me direct the gun towards the water. With a nudge of my finger, the bullets came storming out the barrel, one after another, and each bullet hit the water like a submarine diving into the ocean. He eventually let go and let me shoot on my own. I hear the OGs in the background laughing— saying, "Look at this little Crip busting on the water!" I got so comfortable; I was shooting and yelling, telling the OGs, I would love to smoke a Blood member.

What I learned quickly was the Crips and Bloods didn't get along. Everything was about respect and making sure rival gang members understood each other's territories. If you were on a street that a rival gang claimed, you didn't belong there. If you wanted to pass through or handle some business with someone in that neighborhood, you would need to get permission from the head OG who ran everything on that block. I knew that rolling around with the Crips could get me sent to jail or killed, but I took my chances because living in the Ville was very unpredictable. I didn't want to be somebody's prey—I wanted to be a predator.

My mother tried her best to control me, but I wouldn't listen to her. She would tell me if I hung around the wrong people I might end up in jail or dead. I didn't have a father figure in my life, and when you see your mom struggling financially, day after day, you don't have time to be a child. While most kids had to be home before the streetlights came on, I was out running the streets, trying to make money by any means necessary. My mom often got boxes of food from the church with cereal, government cheese, milk, and canned goods, but it didn't last long because there were a lot of mouths to feed in our home.

I didn't like coming home at night because we hardly had any food, and I had to sleep on the sofa in our roach-infested apartment. The roaches were so bad that when I woke up in the middle of the night, I would have an army of them on my blanket. We couldn't avoid the roach infestation. Even if we used Raid bug spray, laid sticky traps killing some of them, the majority of them would plague our apartment from top to bottom. To this day, I can't stand Corn Flakes because every morning before school, I always had a bowl of Corn Flakes cereal. One day, I poured the cereal in the bowl and then the milk, grabbed my spoon, and sat down at the table in the kitchen. I took one bite, then another, and I felt something moving in my mouth. I spit the cereal back in my bowl to find a huge roach in my bowl! I was so grossed out that from that day on, I never ate Corn Flakes again.

What I loved about the Ville was that many people who were poor and struggling to survive still helped each other, despite their circumstances. We had plenty of friends and neighbors who loved my mom and would give her hand-me-down clothes, shoes, canned foods, and food stamps. My mom would return the favor and do the same for them.

I had many friends in the Ville who always had my back and would do anything for me. It wasn't always about your race or gang affiliation; it was about who would be there for you in your time of need. I spent a great deal of time with my friends Nano and Benny, who were brothers. I was over at their house like it was my house. Their mom and dad always asked me, "Mijo, you hungry?" I was so skinny; I could never turn down a meal. Benny was the oldest brother, and he and Nano would fight like cats and dogs, but at the end of the day, they loved each other. I used to wish I had a biological brother, but *they* were like my brothers, so that filled the empty space I had.

Ameel was another one of my homeboys that lived in the Ville. He was a straight-up, hard-nosed type of kid who welcomed fights. His mom, Ricky, was a sweet lady who befriended my mom. Whenever we needed food or anything else, she was there to help. She tried to control Ameel, but that was like trying to tame a lion. Ameel, Benny, Nano, some other kids, and I would go behind the apartments to a huge dirt field to build forts and have rock fights. We would divide the teams up equally and then go find old slabs of wood and shopping baskets. We would take the wood and lie it up against the basket, so we wouldn't get hit by a rock. We would all collect rocks that were thin and big with sharp edges. I would load my rocks in my shirt, and when I had enough, I laid them by my fort. When everybody had all their rocks, we would yell, "Rock fight!" and start throwing rocks. If you got hit, you were out. I threw a rock at Ameel, and it curved like a heat-seeking missile, hitting Ameel right in the lip, gashing his mouth wide open. All I could hear was Ameel screaming; blood was gushing everywhere. I ran over to Ameel, took off my white shirt, and put it over his mouth. We ran over to his apartment, which was on the second floor in the Ville, and I yelled, "Ricky, Ameel and I were having a rock fight, and I hit him with a rock on his lip." His mom grabbed Ameel, told one of the neighbors to watch her kids, raced to her car, and took Ameel to the hospital. I saw Ameel the next day. His lip was stitched up, and he was in good spirits, talking about when he got healed, he wanted to pay me back. That was Ameel—tough as nails and not backing down for anyone or anything.

As a little boy, I had extremely low self-esteem and didn't feel attractive at all. What I thought looked attractive was seeing other boys who were light-skinned with long hair and light-colored eyes. I felt like I didn't have a chance on earth to be with a pretty girl. I looked at my dark, scarred-up skin, with blotches on my head and short hair, and saw myself as ugly. My mother and grandmother, though, raised us not to be judgmental towards anyone. If we wanted to be with someone from a particular race, we were encouraged to do so.

There was a young Hispanic girl who had just moved into the Ville; her name was Priscilla. To me, she was the most beautiful girl I had ever seen. She had long black hair, dark brown eyes, and a small frame. All I could think of when I saw her was that she would never give me the time of day. I didn't know if it was destiny, but we ended up going to Foothill Elementary School together in Riverside. That gave me more of a chance of being in the same class, so I could get to know her. One day, I saw her standing by my apartment with her friends, so I said, "Hello", and she waved. I walked over to her with my heart beating outside my chest and introduced myself. I said, "My name is Tyree; what's your name?" She replied, "Priscilla." I asked her how long she had lived in the Ville, and she said just a little while. I told her I thought she was very beautiful, and I would like to hang around with her. She looked at me, smiled, and said, "Sure." I couldn't believe a pretty girl like Priscilla was going to allow me to hang out with her. We became good friends, and eventually, I asked her if she would be my girlfriend. She said, "Yes."

While I thought things were looking hopeful with Priscilla, she had a brother who was a year older, and he didn't like her dating outside of her race. He told Priscilla on numerous occasions that she better dump me, or he would beat me up. I often saw him hanging out around our apartment complex with his homeboys, and he would "mad dog" me, throwing up hand gestures as if he wanted to fight. I told Priscilla to tell her brother he better stop disrespecting me, or I would take care of him. Priscilla said she would talk to her brother, but it didn't do any good. I was trying to restrain myself from fighting. I was already fighting so much at Foothill Elementary that my mother had to sit in class with me all day, so I wouldn't fight. Priscilla's brother wouldn't let up from the name-calling, though, and I'd had enough.

One day, I walked over to her apartment and knocked on the door. I told his mom that her son had a problem with me, and I wanted to settle it right then and there. She yelled, "Mijo, get over here!" He walked to the door and saw me standing right in front of his mom. His mom told both of us, "You're going to fight, and after it's done, you're going to shake hands and let it go." We squared up on the front lawn of Priscilla's apartment, and it seemed the whole village came out to watch us fight. He threw a punch and missed; I threw a punch and connected right on his chin. I was skinny, but I was quick, with a lot of power. His mom was yelling at him to hit me, but he kept missing. Priscilla was crying and yelling at both of us to stop, but that wasn't going to happen. I felt like a Golden Glove boxer, pounding his face with a drill until he gave up. His mom told him, "You're not done." But, he said he didn't want to fight anymore. One of the neighbors grabbed me and told me, "It's over — go home." I felt good after winning the fight but also sad because I ruined my relationship with Priscilla. Things were never the same after the fight. She didn't want to talk to me anymore. We grew apart and went our separate ways.

Living in the Ville, you rarely had the privilege of having the pizza man deliver to your home. Most of the time, the driver refused to come into our community because he would get robbed, beaten up, or both. It got so bad, Dominos said they would no longer deliver to the Ville. The only way you could get your pizza was to pick it up yourself.

Inside our cage of rage, every day something crazy was happening. I would see people selling drugs out of their apartment back window, like cars were making stops at a drive-through. If you were a little boy and didn't know about sex, you were definitely going to get educated from seeing prostitutes doing tricks on the quad area in the Ville. Women would wear high heels, with short mini-skirts, fake eyelashes, tons of makeup, and all sorts of wigs, trying to cover up their true identity. I was always out late, and when I would come across a prostitute, my eyes would be popping out, looking at these women who were barely dressed. Pimps would be beating up their girls if they didn't come back with enough money, and most of the guys buying sex would be coked out of their minds. You could get any drug you wanted in the Ville. It was like buying candy at a candy store.

Most people in the Ville, though, were always trying to find a way to better themselves and move out of the Ville. None of us had hardly any money. If you were looking for a hustle to earn some cash, you could sell some of your food stamps and make a quick come-up. Food stamps couldn't be used to pay for your light bill, gas or rent, though, so you did what you needed to do to get by.

I remember a time when one of my homeboys and I were broke. He told me there was an apartment that had an eviction notice on the door, but everything was still in there. We came up with a plan to go through the back window when nobody was looking. We had a security guard in the Ville, but he was one of us, so if something went down, he turned his back and looked the other way. So, we waited 'til it got late, casually walked over to the back of the vacant apartment and slid the window open. He went in first, and I was right behind him. When we got inside, it was like we struck gold. We took whatever was of value to sell—shoes, clothes, and jewelry. My homeboy was zipping through the house like a Greyhound and then yelled to me, "I found some cash!" I can't recall how much it was, but for two broke little kids, that money seemed like a million bucks. We took what we could and went back to our place to divide up the money. I felt kind of bad for taking the money, but I thought, "These people got evicted, so they're not coming back for anything." That was everyday life in the Ville. You did whatever you had to in order to survive.

We had enough drama going on in the Ville as it was, when my mom dropped a bombshell on me, my sisters, and my grandmother—she had a new man. She brought him over to meet our family, and I immediately knew he was bad news. He was Puerto Rican, over six feet tall, with dark hair and glasses. On the outside he looked like a nice man, but to me, he was Public Enemy Number One. He brought my family some chocolate bon-bons, and I thought, "That's a nice gesture, but he's just trying to weasel his way into our family to take over!" It wasn't long before he finagled his way into moving in with us, and none of us were happy about that at all. That nice person my mom thought she was getting, turned into a dictator. He told my mom my grandmother should be in a nursing home, but we would never do that to our grandmother! Even though she wasn't getting around like she used to, my grandmother was the glue that kept our family together. My aunt Betty wasn't happy about his demands, considering he hadn't lived with us long enough to have a clue about our family. My aunt eventually took my grandmother to live with her because she couldn't take this savage man disrespecting my grandmother.

The one thing he did do right was encourage my mother to move out of the Ville. My mother knew the Ville wasn't a good place to live, and she needed to move. But, once my mother got comfortable, she did not like to change her environment. The day we moved out of the Ville was a happy and sad day. I was happy we were leaving our roach-infested apartment, and I didn't have to deal with violence, gangs, drugs, or prostitution anymore—but I was sad to leave my friends behind who stuck by me through thick and thin. The good news was I would see most of my friends in middle school the following school year at Wells Intermediate, in Riverside, CA.

Chapter 3

New Beginnings

We eventually moved out of Montgomery Village to the Shelter Creek apartments, which were about five minutes from my old neighborhood. I didn't have my own room because we couldn't afford a three-bedroom, so I was back on the sofa. But, that was OK, considering we were out of the Ville. By then, I was no longer attending Foothill Elementary School; I was attending Wells Intermediate now. Before school started, I was determined to earn some money to help my mother buy me school clothes, so I walked across the street from my apartment to Howard's Rental which rented equipment. I asked the owner if I could have a job sweeping his lot, and he agreed. I don't remember what he paid me, but it was more than I had. I also had a good friend in my apartment whose dad had a business doing landscaping, so I asked him if he could ask his dad to hire me. His dad replied that I could come to work with them, but there was to be no fooling around — I needed to do an honest day's work.

I was twelve years old and working two jobs. I put in great work and earned the money I needed to help my mom pay for my school clothes. I remember giving my mom the cash; she was so happy and had tears in her eyes. My mom's boyfriend was very jealous, and he tried to take my money to use it for what he wanted. My mom stood up for me, and he backed down. In the early eighties, going to Wells was like living in the Ville. You always had to have your head on a swivel, show no signs of weakness, and if someone wanted to fight, you'd better knuckle up, or you would get labeled a punk. I was starting to mature a lot during my first year of sixth grade. Back in elementary, I would fight almost every day. It got so bad that in the third grade, my mother had to sit in class with me, so I wouldn't fight. That really made me feel embarrassed. What else contributed to my maturation was that I found a new love — playing football. My coaches had high hopes for me. They found out I had been fighting in school, and they told me if I continued to fight I would never amount to anything. I would end up on the street, strung out on drugs, dead, or in jail. I didn't want this to happen.

I fought only a couple more times while I was in seventh grade. The first fight I had was during PE. One of the eighth-grade boys didn't like me, so he said something bad and then swung at me and missed. I swung back, hitting him about three or four times, and then the fight was over. During my last fight, I fought another student in front of my classroom before class. My teacher tried to stop us, but she couldn't; some kids in our class broke up the fight. Those were my last fights, and then I made a huge transition to get my life on track. I signed up for track and football at my middle school, and I excelled in both, playing and beating kids who were older than me. I remember William Jacobsmeyer, our physical education teacher, had us run "timed miles" all the time. Despite my having severe asthma, I would battle with Jose Hernandez, David Becerra, and many others to see who the fastest miler in school was. Coach J, as we called him, was prepping me to be a great runner one day – without my knowing it.

My mom and sisters were surprised at my drastic turn-around in school; I was getting honor roll and student-of-the-week recognition all the time. I would also ride my bike to my friend Jason Ramberg's house in the morning, so we could get tutoring from our history teacher, Mr. Leslie. I loved riding my bike to Jason's house in the morning because he used to tell me, "You can have anything you want from the pantry." I was always hungry because we didn't have a lot of food at home. His parents were always loving to me and treated me like family. I really loved his friendship because he never judged me for being poor; he just accepted me as I was.

My older sister, Rosalyn, also attended Wells with me, and I loved that because she was like my best friend. I would tell her anything and everything. And even when I would get in trouble at school, she would be the one who would forge my mom's signature, so my mom and her boyfriend wouldn't know I got in trouble. But, Rosalyn didn't like it when I would date her friends because once I got tired of them, I would break up with them. Then, they would go tell my sister what I did, and she would yell at me because they said I broke their hearts.

Wells was a lot like the movie *Lean On Me*. We had lots of racial fights, and I remember that many of those fights went on in the bathroom where someone had a butterfly knife and brass knuckles. We had a high turnaround of teachers because if you didn't have thick skin and couldn't handle the pressure of violence, or some student cussing you out, you weren't going to last. Wells was an environment that I can truly say helped me to become tougher. We had Crips, Bloods, Skinheads, and Mexican gangs at our school. I always felt Wells was like a prison, with the teachers as guards, keeping watch over us as if we were the inmates. I was always broke, and most of the students at Wells were the same way. To earn some money, sometimes we would play craps in the bathroom — anywhere secluded where teachers couldn't find us. Another hustle many of us had was buying donut holes and selling them at school for a profit.

There were a lot of good times at Wells in the eighties, too, and I made sure I took advantage of most of them. I recall my first kiss. There was a girl who was very athletic at my school, and most of my friends believed we should be together. Back then, we passed notes to each other to get messages to girls we liked and didn't like. I couldn't face the girl I liked, but I wrote a letter to her friend, telling her friend that I liked her and wanted to kiss her. Students at school said we would be a good couple because we were both athletic and could both really dance. One day, I was walking home from school with my friend Jason Ramberg. We both saw the girl I liked, and Jason said, "Why don't you go over and talk to her?" I did, but I was extremely nervous and felt my heart was going to pop out of my chest. I approached her and couldn't believe how beautiful she was. We had some small talk, and then it was that moment for us to say goodbye. It seemed like it was taking forever. Both of us were waiting for the other one to make the first move to kiss. At the same time, we both leaned forward with our eyes closed, and we kissed. It was a nice little, quick peck on the lips that seemed so pleasant and innocent — and then it was over. I gave her a hug and ran back to Jason. I told him what had happened, and that was it. Oddly, we never became girlfriend and boyfriend, but I will always remember the kiss we had walking home after school that day.

My time at Wells had lots of memorable times, but it all came to an end at the beginning of my eighth-grade year when my mom and boyfriend decided to move to a better area, so I could attend a safer school. It was tough to leave my friends, but I needed a change. I was tired of worrying about getting into trouble with the wrong person and being shanked or stabbed.

Chapter 4

Riverside Junior Tackle Football League

The streets in the 1980s, in Riverside, CA, were like the grim reaper. They took many lives. I was a young boy, full of testosterone, and looking to get in all types of trouble while living in Montgomery Village aka "The Ville." My only safe haven was Bryant Park. It was a place to go when you wanted to feel safe and get fed. My father was non-existent in my life, but God had a plan to put the right men in my life at the right time. Raymond Aguirre was one of those men. He was a recreational leader at Bryant Park in the early '80s. He was a strong, Hispanic man that looked like a Cholo with his black hair slicked back, dark black mustache, and dark brown eyes that could pierce your soul. He didn't take any disrespect from anyone, and he was very respected throughout Riverside. He would give you the shirt off his back, and at the same time, get in your face if you did something wrong because he genuinely cared about you, and wanted the best for you. I was always at the recreational center playing basketball, football, foosball, or pool with my friends. It was a good feeling to know that Raymond, along with the other staff, made sure we had glimpses of normalcy while being at the recreational center. Many of my friends who lived in the Ville didn't have much to eat or drink, but Raymond and the staff would make sure we all had something to eat during our time at the park. Raymond was not just a staff member—he was a surrogate father to me and many boys and girls who made Bryant Park their second home.

There were lots of fights at Bryant Park in the early '80s, and the gang activity was very violent. Raymond, personally, made it his business to let all gangs and gang members know that the recreational center was off-limits for violence and drugs. I, personally, witnessed Raymond break up fights and tell gang members they needed to take their foolishness elsewhere. He was truly sent by God to protect us from harm's way while we were in his care.

The summers at Bryant Park were a special time. Getting free lunch seemed like a gourmet meal to most of us. Every day around noon, Raymond and the staff would grab boxes of food and set them up by the picnic tables that had this huge wooden covering, shaped like an umbrella. If you wanted lunch, you would have to get there early with an adult. My mom was usually with me, along with my two sisters, and we would stand in line and wait for the staff to start serving food. There was a rule you could only get one lunch because there were so many people in need of food. Sometimes, the staff would give me two lunches because they knew we were always short on food. I would save my extra lunch and use it for dinner. I loved those days! I could play *and* fill my little belly up!

One day, I was at Bryant Park, playing as usual on the basketball courts, and I saw some kids at the end of the park playing football. I knew about football, but I had never played on a team. My curiosity took over, and I decided to walk towards the end of the park where all the kids were playing football. When I got there, I saw all these kids wearing helmets, shirts with shoulder pads, and football pants with pads in them. I saw a big man, and he was blowing a whistle, so the kids could run sprints on his command. I assumed he was the coach, so I walked up to him and asked him how I could play football. He said, "If you want to play for the Riverside Junior Tackle Football League, you need your mom or dad to fill out a permission slip and pay one hundred dollars for your football equipment and uniform." I replied that I didn't have a dad, so my mom could sign the permission slip, but we were poor and couldn't afford to pay one hundred dollars. The big man with the hat and shorts and a whistle hanging around his neck, who the players called Coach P., said, "You can sell one hundred raffle tickets, and that will pay for your uniform and football equipment." I thanked the coach, and I ran as fast as I could back to the Ville to tell my mother. When I reached my mom, I was so out of breath, I had to pull out my inhaler. I told her the coach at Bryant Park said I could play football if I sold one hundred raffle tickets. My mom replied, "Boy, you're too small to play football! How are you going to play with them if you can barely breathe?" I responded and told her that I could play and stood there begging until she finally said, "Yes." I believe my mother was actually happy on the inside because now I could use football to channel my anger instead of fighting.

My mother stayed true to her word and signed me up to play football for the Pee Wee Aggies. Coach P. gave us one hundred raffle tickets for discounts from various stores around town. My mother and two sisters agreed to stand with me in front of Vons, Thrifty, and K-Mart to sell tickets. I told my potential buyers, "Hello, ma'am or sir, would you be interested in buying a Riverside Junior Tackle Football League raffle ticket to help pay for my equipment and uniform?" Some bought tickets, and some gave me money and told me to do whatever I wanted with the money. I put the money towards my uniform and equipment because that was one less ticket I had to sell. The tickets were a dollar each, and within one week from the time we got the tickets, we sold all one hundred. It didn't matter how hot it was during that California summer or how late it got, my family stood in front of those stores and sold tickets. I did that every year to pay for my uniform and equipment.

The day I handed Coach P. all one hundred dollars was one of the happiest times in my life. I felt like I was on top of the world. I didn't go steal from anyone or rob anyone. I worked hard for every dollar I received. It was a great feeling—knowing I was part of a team of players, coaches, and team moms who wanted to see me succeed in life. My mother had never driven a car in her life nor had my grandmother or my two sisters. When the coach sent word that all players would have to go pick up their uniform in downtown

Riverside on Chicago Street, I told my coach I didn't have a ride. He said, "Don't worry; I will take you." We went to pick up our helmets, shoulder pads, pants, thigh, hip, and knee pads on a Saturday from an old warehouse in downtown Riverside. I thought we would be the only team there, but there was an army of other football players from different parks throughout Riverside. I stood in line with all my teammates and coaches until we were up next to get fitted for our helmets, shoulder pads, pants, and pads. When I got all my equipment, I couldn't believe I was finally a football player. I took all my equipment home, feeling so proud and accomplished that for the first time in my life I was someone special. I was part of a team and fraternity now, and I wasn't going to let anyone take that away from me.

The Riverside Junior Tackle Football League had many different levels: Pee Wee, Junior Pee Wee, Junior Midget, and Midget. What determined your level was your age and weight. I was so skinny that if the wind blew hard, I would fly away, so I was definitely a Pee Wee. The first day of practice, my coach asked me and my teammates what number we wanted. I chose 23 because it seemed like a good number. When you first start playing football at the Pee Wee stage, coaches will play you at many different positions from offensive line, running back, wide receiver, kicker, etc. Eventually, it became clear I was suited to be a running back, despite my scrawny frame. I was learning about football every day and getting better and better.

Our team moms were the backbone of our team. They made sure we had oranges, drinks, and snacks for every practice and game. My mom was a team mom, and she felt really good being part of a sisterhood who were helping to turn young boys into men. The day before our first game, Coach P. and all the assistant coaches handed out our new jerseys. Our team colors were purple and gold, and boy, did they look awesome! When my coach called my name to get jersey number 23, I lit up like the fourth of July, and everyone could see my excitement. I wore my jersey home, and I couldn't stop looking at it. I felt like a king in all that purple and gold!

My first game playing for the Aggies was crazy. I didn't know what to do and neither did most of my teammates, but we were having fun. We lost our first game, but we learned a lot about the game of football that day. Each game, I became more confident, and my football knowledge increased. Before a game, I would always be scared, but I knew if I didn't put my fears aside and just hit my competitors before they hit me, I would always be scared. I made lots of friends on the Aggies. My friend, Robert Grizzle was bigger than I was, but he could run with the best of us. When we weren't playing football, we were at each other's homes playing pick-up football, playing with his train set, eating donuts, and watching television. My first year playing for the Aggies was a success. I had great coaches who were surrogate dads, and all the team moms were my surrogate moms. I was sad when the football season ended because I was getting better each game. I knew the following year; I would be playing for coach Gil Lake who was the head coach for the Steelers. I heard he was a great coach, and next year's team was going to be a great one!

The following year I was on the Steelers, and it was a far cry from being on Jr. Pee Wee. My sister Rosalyn was a cheerleader, and my mom met some new team moms. Coach Gil Lake was a no-nonsense type of coach who rode you like Zorro but built you up like Fort Knox. He instilled in me important values, such as, respecting my elders, peers, and competitors and being responsible. He knew we would mess up in practice and in games, so he told us to forget about the mistake we made and to move forward by finding a way to fix it. When he spoke, you listened! Just like my former coach, he was all about developing athletes and turning them into great players.

One of his assistant coaches, Butch, I didn't really like at the time. He stayed on me like white on rice. If I messed up on an offensive or defensive play, he was all up in my face. I didn't realize it at the time, but Coach Butch saw a lot of athletic potential in me. That's why he was on me so much to do better every practice and game. I was one of the smaller players on the team compared to everyone, but what I did have was mojo. I had heart. I loved to hit and was fast as lightning.

Coach Lake and the assistant coaches had us primed and ready for the season. Most of us played pick-up football games against other kids from other neighborhoods, did physical education at school, rode bikes from city to city, and raced other kids in the streets, using streetlights as markers to get into football shape. I was fortunate to have some of the most talented teammates in California on my Steelers squad. Taylor played wide receiver and running back, and he was a force to be reckoned with. Rivas wasn't that fast, but he hit like a freight train. Our offensive and defensive line consisted of the Compton twins and Jeremy, who regularly put people on their backs.

There was a lot of competition that year, and one of our rivals, who had a talented squad, was the Reid Park Trojans. Every year, it didn't matter what division you were playing in; the Trojans always brought their A game. At the end of the season, it was the Steelers against the Trojans in the Super Bowl. There was lots of hard hitting and trash talking, with scores going back and forth. The Trojans knew I was fast and loved to hit, so they would try to double-team me as much as they could to keep me isolated from any play they were running. Every time I ran the football, they would try to knock me out, but they didn't know the more they hit me, the more I got fired up to want to take them out one by one. In the end, we had more mojo than they did, and we won the Super Bowl. That was my first ever Super Bowl win playing in the Riverside Junior Tackle Football League, and I was on cloud nine.

Playing for the RJTFL was a blessing. There were so many great coaches, players, team moms and dads. We played most of our games at different parks throughout Riverside. I remember playing a lot of my games at Ramona High School. I would arrive early before my game and watch other teams play. One Saturday, the Midget division had a game, and it was the Cowboys vs the Jets. The game seemed to be going great until one of the players got hit after the whistle was blown. Suddenly, all hell broke loose. Players were fighting, throwing punches, and using their helmets as weapons.

Then, the parents who were watching the game, left the sidelines, and they were fighting each other. Our coaches ran over and told us to get back. It was pandemonium everywhere! I know football is a gladiator sport, but when it escalates to the point where players are taking their helmets off to hit one another, that's when you have disrespected the league, players, and family members who are watching.

When one football season came to an end, another began. My new team was the Riverside Rams. Coach Beard was our head coach and offensive coordinator, and Coach Maier was our defensive coordinator. Coach Beard was a high energy type of coach, and Coach Maier was laid-back but stern. Our team loved Coach Beard's enthusiasm, and we adopted his enthusiastic mindset the whole year while practicing and playing against our competitors. Our team was loaded with talent. I played free safety and running back; Taylor played wide receiver. RB was our quarterback, and Smalls was another one of our running backs. We ran through our opponents all year like paper walls. Our offense was so in sync and disciplined, we rarely gave up points. My goal was to score every time I touched the football, and I did that most of the time. When I was on defense, I made sure to hit my opponents like a Mack truck. My first season being with Coach Beard was great! We went undefeated and won the Super Bowl. The second year we demolished every one of our competitors and only allowed our opponents to score nineteen points on us the whole season. Because we dominated every team and beat them so handily, the league officials had a meeting to arrange for our team to play another undefeated team in Phoenix, AZ.

The day of the game I was nervous as always but eager to score touchdowns and give many licks to my competitors. Coach Beard and the assistant coaches took us all out on the field for the pregame; hearing the music playing and looking over at our competitors had me pumped up. When the pregame was over, we all walked over to the sideline, and the referee blew the whistles for the captains to walk out. Smalls, Taylor, RB, and I were captains. We called, "Heads" and lost the toss, so we had to kick off. We kicked off, and our special teams did their job and made the tackle on the forty-yard line. The first play, the other team ran sixty yards for a touchdown because we had a busted coverage, and boy, did that light a fire in our team. I scored on the opening kickoff and ran ninety-nine yards for a touchdown. My touchdown put us back in the game. The game went back and forth with many touchdowns scored, but as the time on the clock started to wind down, we started to wear down our competitors on both offense and defense. We had too many weapons, and our competitors were over-matched. The final score was 38-16. We finished our Cinderella season undefeated, bringing another title back to the Riverside Junior Tackle Football League.

Chapter 5

La Sierra High School

I had just graduated from middle school, and now it was time to prepare for high school. My mother and her boyfriend decided we should move closer to my high school because it was going to be a long four years, going to school and playing sports. We moved to the Heritage Apartments, which was literally ten minutes walking distance from La Sierra High School, and I loved that. Our new apartment had three bedrooms, so I would have my own room, which was a luxury. Another plus was one of my football buddies, Mike Acedo, lived in the same apartments with his mom, Annette, and his stepdad, Edmundo. Mike was a good football player and a friend. His family was like my family, and I was a regular at his house because he lived downstairs from me.

Freshman orientation was the summer of 1991. We got our class schedule and learned what classes we would be taking. The football coaches, from freshman to varsity, laid out the agenda for all players. If you wanted to play freshman football, you needed to complete a medical packet and make sure you passed a physical.

The freshman football coaches already knew about me from talks around town and my performance with the Riverside Junior Tackle Football League. They were licking their chops. They knew I was a blazer, that I could score almost every time I touched the football, and was great at defense, too. Mike and I were excited to play football. Our freshman coaches told us we would have summer practice in the morning and in the evening to get us in shape for the upcoming season.

I had never done two-day workouts, but I knew it would make me better. The first football session with Coach Enyart was in the weight room. I had never lifted weights, but I had done lots of sit-ups and push-ups. The weight room was in the back of the school right next to the swimming pool. When I walked into the weight room, it reeked of sweat, and the weights seemed to be rusty and ancient. The coaches talked often about the many great athletes who came before us, and the football players who still came to use the gym to get better every day. I was very motivated to start lifting weights after the coaches gave us insight on how to become bigger, stronger, faster, and better athletes.

We did circuit training in the weight room, and I started off with bench. I was so skinny, and it seemed like the bar weighed more than me. The coaches put ninety-five pounds on the bench, and it took all my might to do one rep. Our coaches were trying to find out our max in the bench press, power clean, and military press, so we could know how many times we could lift that weight. Every day, I got a little stronger, faster, and bigger. We had lots of great potential on our freshman football team. Some of my freshman teammates looked like grown men, including Jorge and Gary, who both had beards. My good friend, Aaron, was green at playing football and would always have a hard time catching the football, so my coaches named him "long ball" because you could send him on a deep route, but most likely, he wasn't going to catch it. I had a great feeling our freshman team was going to devour our competition when the season started in a month or so.

After summer training was over, or as the coaches called it, "Hell Week," Coach Enyart and the rest of the coaches came up with a starting lineup. I was going to play running back and free safety. I loved my positions because I loved to run the ball and score touchdowns, and I also loved to hit. My motto was, "Hit everything in sight that moves on the opposing team."

The night before my first day of school, everything had to be in order. I made sure I ironed my new clothes and set my shoes and backpack by the door. My hair was freshly cut into a flat-top. I could barely go to sleep that night, and the morning came quick! I got up early, and my mom was already up making sure I had everything I needed. I ate some breakfast, got dressed, and then went downstairs to Mike's apartment to knock on his door. He was all dressed up and ready to head out for our first day at La Sierra High School. It was the beginning of September, and the sun was beaming early in the morning while Mike and I walked to school. When I walked onto campus, the school and students looked so huge. Mike and I were fresh fish, and the seniors ruled the school.

I heard a lot of talk about our varsity players, Byron, Chauncey, Jeff, Sammy, and Jabbar. They were La Sierra legends in football; everyone seemed to know them and worshipped the ground they walked on. I got the chance to talk to Byron and Chauncey, and they were very encouraging. I hoped one day I'd be in their shoes, being a big-time football player at La Sierra. That's what I wanted to be—one of the greatest football players to come out of La Sierra, but there was lots of work to be done. If I wanted to play football at a major university, I definitely needed to be around players who were better than me, so I could be pushed to become great. I also made sure I took challenging classes my freshman year, so I would be on track to get a full-ride scholarship to play football at a Division 1 university after my senior year.

Our first game was the first week of school, and I was ready. We dominated our opponents. For the season, Jake played quarterback, Deandre and I were running backs, and Mike played tight end. Our defense was solid as a rock, and we didn't allow many points scored on us all year from our competition. I loved it when the varsity players came to watch us play. I wanted to put on a show, so they knew all the rumors they heard about me being fast, hitting hard, and scoring from anywhere on the football field were true. I did put on a show many times in front of the varsity coaches and players, and I gained lots of respect and recognition. My season was going great until I suffered a severe asthma attack from smog inhalation.

Riverside, during the summer, has some of the worst air quality, and I paid the price by being admitted to ICU for a week. I was so frustrated I couldn't practice or play, but I knew my teammates would fill the void. I spent a week in ICU laid up in a hospital bed, getting breathing treatments and steroid shots to open my lung passages.

Finally, I was cleared to go back to practice, and it felt great to be back! I finished out my freshman season being one of the team's star players, and that was a great accomplishment in my book.

My freshman banquet was at the end of the season, and I was asked to be one of the speakers to give an award to the coaches. One of our coaches told me to address Coach Enyart, Sr. as, "Old Man Enyart." I stood in front of the podium and thanked all the coaches for a wonderful season. I then asked if Old Man Enyart would come up and accept his award. Everyone in the room laughed like it was the funniest joke on planet earth. I gave the coach his award and walked back to my seat. One of the assistant coaches said, "I can't believe you actually said it." It was all in love, and Coach Enyart, Sr. knew that.

I loved playing football with my boys, and I was happy my best friend, Mike, was right there with me every step of the way. My mom was extremely happy that I was doing well in football and school, but her boyfriend was extremely jealous. He didn't like that I was playing sports. I didn't get along with him at all. He abused my mother to the point where she would be screaming in the bedroom. My older sister Rosalyn and I would bang on the door to tell him to let go of our mom but trying to get him off her was like a gnat hitting an elephant. Whenever he was drinking or drugged-up, he was a very violent man. I knew the only way I could help my mom and sisters was to get myself together and get a scholarship, so I could take them away from him.

When things got really bad, I went downstairs to Mike's house, so I wouldn't end up fighting. I spent many days at Mike's house playing video games like Techno Bowl and John Madden on his Genesis. We played games all day and night when we didn't have anything else to do. I was a sore loser at times and would go off on Mike, but he would brush it off because he knew I had a good deal of rage because of my family situation.

The following spring, I ran track. I thought of it as a means to an end to get in shape for football. I knew if I wanted to become more appealing to football scouts, I needed to be in two sports and be dominant in both. As a freshman, I ran the 100-meter, 200-meter, and the 4X100m relay on the varsity team. I had to win a spot on the relay by racing against our starting varsity running back, Byron. He had the spot I wanted, so our head varsity coach, Dwight Berry said, "Why don't you two do a race-off?" We set the distance for one-hundred meters, and I beat him. Byron was shocked a freshman took his spot on the relay. The whole school eventually found out I beat Bryon. I was going to be the only freshman running on the varsity sprint relay team. I was happy because I was going to get my varsity letter as a freshman. I was the runt on the relay. Our squad made it all the way to the California Interscholastic Finals (CIF) that year, but we didn't medal. I gained a great deal of experience by racing varsity athletes from other schools and participating in invitationals throughout California, which made me a better football player the following football season.

The summer of 1992 I was getting primed and ready for another great football season in the fall. I was moved to the varsity roster my sophomore year. To kick off the summer, we would have passing league for about a month, and we played twenty games within that time frame. It was a good time for me to get some reps in with my varsity teammates, so I could work on my defensive and receiver skills. Passing league helped me shake off the cobwebs and build unity with my teammates. When the first week of August arrived, it was D-Day for all the junior and varsity players. We were issued our football equipment, and I knew then— it was game on. Hell Week was starting, and all the coaches were going to be our drill sergeants for a week. We still had two workout sessions—one in the morning and one in the evening.

Mike and I were at home, eating and resting before our first practice. I had the tendency, though, to eat too much and would feel bloated and heavy. I knew if I went to practice feeling that way, it would affect my performance. So, I went in the bathroom, closed the door, and turned on the water and the vent, so my mom and sisters couldn't hear what I was doing. I stuck my hand down my throat and threw up. After I was done, I looked in the mirror and noticed my eyes had a glossy/watery look, but I felt great. I no longer felt heavy or bloated, and I could go to practice feeling good. I thought it would be a one-time thing, but over the next few weeks, I repeated this practice.

My sister cornered me one day as I was coming out of the bathroom. She asked me why my eyes were so glossy, and I replied it was because I had something in my eye, and I had to wash my eye. She told me I was lying, and that I was in the bathroom again, throwing up. I couldn't believe she was stalking me and knew almost every time I went into the bathroom to throw up. She threatened if I didn't stop, she would tell my mom. I didn't want that, so I told her I would stop to shut her up. But, I knew I was getting great results throwing up my food before practice and games, so why should I stop?

My first workout as a varsity player was an intense weight room circuit where we would bench, power clean, squat, then grab forty-five-pound plates, and walk around the weight room. We would also have to squat against the wall to burn out our quadriceps and then run a lap on the dirt track. Players were throwing up their breakfasts; some were nearly passing out, and others who couldn't "hack it"—tapped out for good. Coach Hank Moore, Coach Dwight Berry, and the other assistant coaches were trying to weed out the weak because only the strongest were going to survive. I loved being challenged because, for me, it was about winning small victories and getting better every day. I was a perfectionist, and everything I did had to be flawless, with no room for error. When Bryon came to practice, he wore matching shorts, wrist bands, and sleeves rolled up with a cut-off shirt to show off his muscles and abs. I asked him why he came to practice like that, and he said, "If you look good, you practice and play good." I took that advice and ran with it. Of course, I wanted to perform, but I wanted to perform, looking good.

My sixteenth birthday was August 28, 1992. The first-team offense was going against the first-team defense. I was rotating in and out at Z-back because we ran a wing-T offense. I scored twice on the first-team defense, and Coach Moore was yelling at the defense to stop me. When I went in for the third time, Jeff, who was our starting quarterback and stood about 6'5," told everyone to huddle up, so he could give us the play to run. I knew the ball was coming to me, so I was ready. Jeff walked up to the line and placed his hands under the center. All eleven offensive players were lined up, and Jeff gave the count. The ball snapped, and Jeff turned to hand the ball to me. One defender after another tried to hit me, but I'm shaking and baking. Then, I made a quick decision to go up the middle and jump. Sammy, who was 6'2" and 240 pounds, hit me while I tried to jump over the middle to score, and he delivered a mighty blow, stopping me in my tracks. I didn't score. I picked myself off the ground. I could hear Coach Moore yelling, "Good run, Ty, and good hit, Sammy!" As I walked back to the huddle, I felt my shoulder drop, so I told Coach Berry that my shoulder was probably broken. He and Coach Moore stopped practice and looked at my shoulder. Sure enough, my coaches said it was probably broken. I remember Sammy walking over to me and saying he was sorry. I told him it was okay because if I were on the opposite side, I would have hit him the same way. The coaches called my mom and her boyfriend and broke the news that most likely I had broken my collarbone, and they needed to take me to the emergency room right away.

My mom and her boyfriend picked me up and took me to the hospital. It didn't take long to be seen by an emergency room doctor. The doctor sent me to get X-rays. After his evaluation, the doctor told me I had a partial break in my clavicle. He said I wouldn't need surgery, but I would be in a brace for about two months. I was devasted because I thought my season was over. My goal was to leave high school with a scholarship, and if I missed games, it would lessen my chances of being seen by college recruiters.

I went to the Riverside Sports Clinic early in the morning with one of my varsity teammates, Nash, who had a sore hamstring. My rehab consisted of exercises to strengthen my collarbone, ultra-sound treatments, and ice. At about the two-month mark, I became very impatient to see if my collarbone was getting stronger. I would do push-ups in my room. My sister Rosalyn would tell me, "You're not going to heal if you keep aggravating the injury." I didn't care because I wanted to get stronger and get back to my team. I hated going to school in a brace, watching practice, going to the game, and watching from the sidelines. After two months, I was reevaluated by the doctor. He told me I was healed, but I needed to take it easy. I smiled at him, thinking in the back of my head, "As soon as I suit up again with my full uniform, I'm going to go full throttle."

My first day back to practice, Coach Moore and Coach Berry told me that before I got into full uniform, I had to get my shoulder taped. They made a donut out of one of the knee pads and taped it on my clavicle. The coaches bought me some spider shoulder pads, which were a cushion that went under my regular shoulder pads. My first practice back we were scrimmaging, and I took a hit—all was good. That was a confidence builder for me because I knew that when I played in a game, if I got hit, I would be fine.

The week of my first game, I was extremely nervous. I was talking to my best friend, Mike, and sharing with him how many interceptions, tackles, and touchdowns I wanted to have. Going to school was great because doing schoolwork and homework kept my mind off our game a little. But, the anticipation of waiting was nerve-wracking. I was hoping my mom and sisters were going to make my game at the end of the week. That was always a last-minute decision because of my mom's boyfriend's mood swings.

My mother's boyfriend hated that I was doing something I was good at. I hated being at home with my mom's boyfriend because he was a drunk, a drug addict, and he abused my mom. He would get drunk, take some of my mom's disability money, and go buy alcohol and drugs. When he didn't have money, he would force me to go dig in the trash for cans to recycle. When we thought it couldn't be any worse, he made me dig in the trash for food at the 7-11 and grocery stores by our apartment. I would yell at him, I wasn't going to do it, but he would overpower me and make me do what he wanted. My mom was helpless—scared to death that her boyfriend would beat her and all of us if we didn't do what he wanted. We didn't need to dig in the trash for food. We had food at home. Mom may have had little money, but we had enough to get by.

I was always paranoid one of my fellow students might see me digging in the trash. I would be laughed at for the remainder of my high school days at La Sierra. Thank God, no one ever saw us digging in the trash, and if they did know about it, no one said anything. Maybe, it was out of respect because I was a popular athlete at school. I desperately wanted to confide in my coaches, teachers, or the principal, but I knew if I did, they would be mandated to report my mom to Child Protective Services. I didn't want to be taken away from my mom, leaving her with that lunatic. The only way I could release all my frustration and anger was in sports. Football was a great outlet to channel my frustration and anger, by hitting and tackling, without going to jail for assault. My mom was a fighter, and she did her best every day to try and keep our family together, despite the constant beatings she took. Some days when I got home from school, my sisters would tell me my mom was in her room crying and screaming because her boyfriend was beating her. I would bang on the door and tell him to leave my mom alone, but he would keep hitting her until she gave him what he wanted—money. I cussed him out, called him every bad name in the book, and threatened to kill him, but fighting him was a no-win situation because of his size. I wanted him dead, and if he did die, I wouldn't have shed a tear. Mike's parents would hear all the ruckus with my mom and her boyfriend, and sometimes they came up and asked if everything was okay. They always wondered why my mom didn't leave him. He had no job, no money, and without us, he had nowhere to live. Aunt Betty, Uncle Howard, and our friends wanted my mom to leave, but he threatened her if she did leave, he would find her. I believe fear kept my mom in her abusive relationship. The only way out of the situation was if he went to jail, or if he died.

Playing varsity my sophomore year—football was going great. I got some playing time in, on offense and defense, behind the starters. I had one extremely embarrassing moment while we were up in Big Bear, CA, playing another high school called Rim of the World. We were hammering them on both sides of the ball. In one series, we were driving them down the field, and I was on the sidelines, watching our team's every move. We get to the one-yard line, and Coach Moore yells out, "Ty, get in!" My teammates started yelling and clapping because they knew, and I knew, it was pretty much an automatic score. I ran to the huddle, and Jeff Maier, our starting quarterback, gave out the play. We all ran out and got into formation. I lined up right behind Jeff, and my heart was pounding like crazy. I looked at the defense, and the play was for me to run straight ahead, right between the center and the guard. Jeff gave the count; the ball was snapped, and I ran like a bat out of hell, straight ahead to where I was supposed to be. Jeff turned to give me the football. It hit my side because I ran too fast and didn't hesitate for a second, so Jeff could put the ball right on my navel. I fumbled, and we recovered it. I ran back to the sidelines, cussing at myself, embarrassed, and furious that I blew an easy touchdown on the one-yard line. Coach Moore was cool, calm, and collected. He told me, "Shake it off. It's done, and we can't go back in time." I wish I could have because that was going to be my first touchdown as a varsity player. I learned a lot that game. Despite how hard you train and watch film to figure out your opponent's every move, sometimes things don't go the way you planned. You have to keep pushing forward, evaluate what you did wrong, so you can fix it, and hope you don't make the same mistake twice.

We finished the varsity season five and five, which wasn't what we wanted, but it was a great stepping-stone for my junior year. I couldn't help but think about the upcoming track season, but more importantly, my junior year of playing football. I enjoyed track and field, but football was my everything. I wasn't looking to get a track and field scholarship at all, but it did help to be in great shape for football.

Coach Dwight Berry was our head coach for the 1993 track and field season. We didn't have a great deal of talent, but Coach Berry did a phenomenal job putting the right athletes in the right events. This allowed us to score maximum points to win head-to-head track meets and invitationals. My '93 season started off great. I went to the Sunkist Invitational and won the long jump in the high school division. Coach Berry and I were extremely excited about my victory. Even better, I saw Carl Lewis, the Olympic champion, in the hundred meters and long jump, walking around the stadium! I was afraid to go up and ask for an autograph, but Coach Berry encouraged me to go up to him, and I did. I told Carl he was one of my favorite athletes, and I wanted to jump far like him one day.

We went to many track and field invitationals that year, but the one that stood out to me was the Palm Springs Relays. Our team qualified to run in this meet, and that was a big deal for us. We didn't have much talent, but we worked hard. Palm Springs, during the spring, was usually hot and windy. As a team, we did great, scoring enough points to win the meet overall. I finished the '93 track season, winning the league in the long jump. Our 4x400m relay team also won the league. I qualified to compete in the California Interscholastic

Federation Championships in the long jump and 4x400m relay. Unfortunately, I didn't advance in the long jump to the next round nor did our 4x400m relay. Although my season didn't turn out the way I wanted it to, I was happy with the learning experience and my accomplishments.

Every year—the cycle repeated itself. I ran track, then came passing league in the summer, and ended it with Hell Week in preparation for the upcoming football season. As I got a little older, time seemed to pass by faster and faster. The only thing I could think about was getting a four-year scholarship to a Division 1 university, so I could play football, get my degree, and hopefully (Lord willing), get drafted by an NFL team, so I could get my mom and sisters away from her boyfriend.

Despite all the chaos in my life, I knew I had to have a great junior football season. We had a solid team, with many great players like Ron who played quarterback, DeAndre and Mike who played tight end, Brad who played running back, the twins Matt and Bryan, and me. Coach Moore and Coach Berry always made it clear that our goal as a team was to win the Sunkist League and become CIF champions. We didn't win league my junior year, because one of our rivals, Yucaipa High School, edged us out, which made us runner-up in the Sunkist League. We earned a spot to play in the CIF Division 8 Playoffs to play Montebello Cantwell at Riverside Community College.

When the season came to an end, I was pleased about how everything ended. I received letters from major Division 1 universities all over the country. I knew one of my biggest obstacles would be passing my SAT and ACT exams. I was good friends with Coach Berry's daughter, Angelyn. She offered to tutor me, so I would go over to Coach Berry's house and get tutored by Angelyn. It's crazy how things turned out between me and Coach Berry. When I first met him, during my sophomore year, I felt he was always on me with, "Ty, you didn't do this right," or "You should study the playbook more and learn the plays." I couldn't stand Coach Berry when we first met. I thought he was brought here by Satan to ruin my life. Little did I know, he was on me so much because he saw so much potential in me. He believed I could receive a full-ride scholarship to play football and run track at the

Division 1 level. I realized he was on me so much because he cared for me a lot.

Track and Field season was going to start in a couple of months. Coach Berry was going to be the head track coach again, and I was excited. My goal was to win league in the 400m, long jump, and 4X100m relay. After our football banquet, I took a little time off to rest, but I was back in training after two weeks. I spent the offseason running forty-yard sprints, lifting weights, and working with my long jump coach, Chris Reid, to work on my steps for the long jump.

Things at home were heating up between me and my mom's boyfriend. I wasn't the little kid any more who couldn't defend myself. Now, I could fight back. I was seventeen years old. I was lifting weights, getting bigger and stronger, and my fear level of him was at zero. One day, when I was at school, I made the decision to get a gun, so I could kill him. He had hit and abused my mom and sisters one too many times. I knew plenty of people I could get a gun from. Mike Passalacqua, who was a freshman at the time, saw me sitting down on a bench by myself by the classrooms. He asked me if I was okay, and I said, "Yes, I'm good." He asked me again if I was okay, and I said, "Not really." He said, "Let's talk." I asked him if I could tell him something in confidence, and he said, "Yes." So, I told him about my plan to get a gun and kill my mom's boyfriend. He said that wouldn't be a good idea, and that things would get better. I said they would not get better unless I killed my mom's boyfriend. The bell rang for all of us to go to class, and I told Mike to make sure he didn't tell anyone what I was going to do.

For the remainder of school day, I was as silent as a mouse. The school bell rang for the last period, and out of nowhere, Coach Berry and Coach Moore approached me and said, "Mike told us what you were planning to do." I was so upset because I really wanted to kill the guy, so my mom and my sisters wouldn't have to feel pain anymore. Both of my coaches said, "If you kill your mom's boyfriend, your whole future will be thrown away, and you will never be able to play football again." They also told me my mom would be devasted that I was in jail and couldn't be with her and my sisters. I sat there furious, listening to my coaches. I still wanted to kill my mom's boyfriend, and I didn't care what they were saying. Coach Moore and Coach Berry said that Coach

Passalacqua and his wife, Debbie, would allow me to stay with them until I graduated. I felt sad and happy at the same time. I didn't want to leave my mom and sisters, but I knew if I wanted to help them, that first, I would need to help myself.

After track practice, Coach Passalacqua drove me to my house, and I walked in to hug my mom and said, "Hello" to my sisters. Then, I walked into my room and started packing my clothes. My mom asked me what I was doing, and I said, "I'm moving out to go live with my football coach." My mom's boyfriend didn't hear what I was doing until my mom got louder and started crying, telling me not to leave. I told my sisters I was leaving, and they couldn't believe it. I walked out of the door. My mom's boyfriend was yelling at me to get back in the house. I told him, "If I don't leave, I will kill you." He said, "You're not going to kill me!" We both started yelling back and forth, cussing at each other. My mom and sisters came to the door crying, telling me not to leave, but my mind was already made up. If I didn't leave, my future would be over, and one of us would be dead. He yelled at me again and said he was going to call the cops. I said, "Go ahead because I will tell them about how you beat my mom and do drugs." As I walked away, I told my mom and sisters I loved them, and that I would be back to get them away from him. My mom and sisters kept pleading with me to stay, but her boyfriend realized," I better let him go, or he's going to put me in jail." I was scared, heartbroken, and nervous but felt relieved that the Passalacqua family was giving me a fresh start on life.

I moved into the Passalacqua family home during the spring of my junior year. It was a tough transition—leaving my mom, moving to a new home, juggling school and football, but it all worked out for the best. Dan and Debbie treated me like I was one of their sons. I had to do chores and observe a curfew. Dan and Deb took me shopping for clothes and made sure my room was well put together. I tried communicating with my mom and sisters, but it was hard, with my mother's boyfriend playing bodyguard. It was hard for my mom to understand why I left, but she knew it was for the best.

I continued to struggle with my eating disorder. Like lifting weights and practicing football, it was part of my normal routine to eat food and throw it up. I wasn't about to let anything get in the way of my performance and getting a scholarship. Debbie, Dan, Tim, and Mike had no clue what was going on with my eating disorder, and I made it my priority to keep it a secret.

My season went as planned. I dominated my competitors in league meets and in all the track and field invitationals I went to. Coach Berry did a great job again by leading our boys' team to an undefeated season. I won league in the 400m and long jump. I qualified for CIF in all my events, and I ran the 400m in the first round of the CIF championships the following week. I dominated the CIF prelims and the CIF finals in the 400m and long jump.

Coach Berry's and Coach Reid's plan was to get me to win state in both of my events, and everything seemed like it was working out just the way we wanted. I arrived at the masters meet with my coaches and was ready to take out all my competition. I knew I was the champ, and they were going to need to jump their absolute best to beat me. My first jumps were over twenty-three feet, and I felt good. I was confident not too many would be jumping that distance. The anticipation of waiting and watching other jumpers, made my stomach turn at times, but I had to remind myself to stay confident. I was able to hang on for the victory to advance to state.

I was grateful for my victory, but my moment was short-lived because I had to run the 400m in an hour or so. I rested for a little while, made sure I stayed hydrated, and then I went to the warm-up area to prepare for my 400m. I did my normal routine and got up a good sweat. Then, Coach Berry came and said it was time to go to the call area to get my number and lane. I walked back over to where I had put my shoes, and they were not there! I told my coach, and we started asking other coaches and athletes if someone mistakenly took my shoes, and they all said, "No." We were running out of time. I couldn't borrow anyone's shoes to run in, so I had to run in my red Puma long jump shoes.

I was so upset and angry that my shoes suddenly disappeared. I went to the call area to get my number, and I began to sense that one of the runners or their coaches had something to do with taking my shoes. But, I couldn't focus on that. My focus had to be on qualifying and moving on to state. So, I got on the track to do some quick thirty-meter sprints with my long jump spikes on. It felt weird, but I just had to imagine I had my 400m spikes on. The starter then blew the whistle, informing all of us to get behind our blocks. At this point, my heart was racing a mile a minute. Then, the starter said, "Runners, take your mark, set, go."

As I took off out of the blocks, I felt no type of push or bounce. I was watching the other runners take off like race cars. Instead of panicking, I cruised the first 200m, keeping within striking distance. When I hit the next 200m, I was going to make my move. I tried with all my might to pick up the pace, but my shoes were not giving me any push back at all. I came around the last homestretch and finished fourth. I didn't qualify, and my season in the 400m was over.

I was visibly upset and had tears running down my face. I wasn't upset I lost, but that someone had the audacity to take my shoes right before my race. Coach Berry gave me a hug and told me I did the best I could do with what I had. When I returned to the warm-up area, lo and behold, my track spikes were lying right against the fence! Coach and I looked at each other in disbelief because we knew right then, someone had stolen my track spikes to prevent me from qualifying for state. We couldn't file a complaint because we didn't have proof who did it. But, we both knew that one of the runners I was competing against must have had their coach, teammate, family, or friend steal my shoes. My coaches always told me to have a short-term memory, because if something bad happened, you couldn't go back in time and fix it, but you *could* focus on the here and now. I took that advice, and I put all my anger and rage into training, so I could be state champion in the long jump the following week at Cerritos College.

The day before my event, I was extremely nervous because I wanted everything to be perfect. I could hardly sleep, but I made sure I had my uniform, long jump spikes, socks, backpack, and my water. We took the hour drive to Cerritos College, and when we arrived, the stadium was packed with spectators, reporters, camera crews, and athletes from all over California. We arrived on schedule, and my coaches took me to get my packet with my bib number and credentials. I tried to stay calm, but my nerves raged like a wild animal. We had plenty of time before I had to jump, so I had the unusual pleasure of watching the boys' and girls' 4X100m relay.

Time flew by, and it was time for me to warm up. My coaches and I went to the warm-up area, and they guarded my long jump spikes very carefully. The day was clear skies and sunny, and to me, that meant it was going to be a great day. My warmup was superb. I was ready, and I believed no one was going to stop me from winning the state title in the long jump. I wasn't the first jumper, and that was cool because I could sit back and watch what everyone else was jumping.

When my turn came, I walked over to my marker on the runway and took a good stare at the pit. I closed my eyes and saw myself jumping before I jumped. Out of respect, the crowd became silent, so all I could hear was the slight wind caressing my face and my heart beating. I stood there, doing an uppercut motion with my arms a couple of times, and then I took off like a Maserati down the runway. I placed my foot six inches before the board, and I jumped—flying through the air, hitting the sand. I walked out of the pit, waiting for the field judge to put up my mark. I jumped over twenty-three feet, which was a good opener. The crowd that had been silent came roaring back like a tsunami, and I felt good.

All the jumpers went back and forth until I had one more jump left. I was in third place at the time. I waited patiently for my last jump and watched all the other jumpers do their routines and jump in the pit. My final jump was up, and I walked to the runway, knowing it was all or nothing. I walked on the runway and closed my eyes. I stood there thinking about all my training, all the pain I'd endured in my personal life, and all the competitions I'd traveled to, to prepare me for this moment. I opened my eyes, and it seemed as if there was no one in the stadium but me, my coaches, the pit, and the person who would be marking my jump. I stormed down the runway, with each one of my strides ripping up the track. I slightly hit my mark, jumping in the air, pumping my arms, and kicking my legs. Then, I hit the sand and rolled out the back end. I waited for my mark, and it seemed like it took forever. Finally, the field judge raised the white flag to indicate it was a legit jump. My mark comes up, and I see that I jumped 23-9. I was on the leaderboard. I was so happy, but the celebration couldn't start just yet because there were more jumpers to come. I looked over to my coaches and pumped my fist. Now—the waiting game.

I sat there and watched one jumper after another, and I was still in the lead. There were a couple of jumpers left—Jamaal and Jesus—who both had one final jump, but they both scratched on some big jumps, which left me number one on the leader board. The final jumpers didn't come close to my mark, and then the party began. All the jumpers came over to congratulate me. I shook the field judge's hand to thank him for his service, and then over the loud speaker, I listened to the words I'd been waiting to hear the whole season, "The new state champion in the long jump is Tyree Washington, from Riverside, La Sierra High School." The crowd erupted with joy. Coach Reid, Coach Berry, Dan, Debbie, and administrators from my school were there to support me on that historic day. I was so happy, but there was sadness lingering through my thoughts because my mom and sisters weren't with me. I knew my road to success wouldn't come easy, and I also knew I'd have to sacrifice being with my mom and sisters if I wanted to get my life right to help them.

When it was time to get my award, I walked over to the podium and stood on top to receive my gold medal. I smiled from cheek to cheek. I was a state champion, and that would stay with me for the rest of my life. I met my coaches at the warm-up area, and they gave me a big hug. I was so happy they were proud of me because, to me, they were more than coaches—they were my surrogate dads. It took a team effort for me to become a state champion, and if it hadn't been for my coaches and the Passalacqua family, I might never have been standing on that podium receiving my state champion gold medal. It was a great feeling to know that my track and field season was a huge success.

Chapter 6

West Valley Eagles

After competing successfully at the state meet in the long jump, I received a great opportunity to compete for the West Valley Eagles—a renowned track club in Los Angeles. I was approached by the coach and told we would have an elite squad with some of the best sprinters in California. Many great athletes, either were running for the West Eagles, or had run for them in the past. The track club was basically an all-star team of athletes throughout California. I saw what the other players were doing on a national level, and I was sold. So, the summer of 1994, I signed on to run for the West Valley Eagles Track Club.

My concern, though, was whether I'd be able to afford my uniform, spikes, and travel expenses. Thankfully, it ended up all being covered through sponsorships. That was comforting, considering my family was on welfare, and my mom wasn't working because she was on disability. Coach Howard assembled a 4X400m relay team that was amazing. We had Patrick, who was the state champion in the 100m and 200m; Bryan, who was the state champion in the 100m; I was the state champion in the long jump, and Michael, who had one of the fastest times in the nation in the 400m.

Our first competition was at the National Scholastic Outdoor Championships at North Carolina State University. I had never been on a plane before, so it was going to be quite the experience for me. Roger Lipkis was another one of our coaches. He worked with the Olympic champion, Quincy Watts, and many other great former West

Valley Eagles' athletes. We didn't have to worry about uniforms, plane tickets, hotel expenses, food, or transportation. Sponsorship took care of everything we needed. All we had to do, as athletes, was focus on running fast and winning our races.

The day of the 4X100m relay, my team ran a blistering time of 40.55, winning the National Scholastic Championships and breaking the meet record. After a great performance in the 4X100m relay, we also won the 4X400m relay. That team which included Patrick, Michael G., Michael R., and I, ran a blazing time of three minutes and seven seconds. I was so happy my first competition, out-of-state, was not only a huge success, but it confirmed; I could compete with the best sprinters in the US. We celebrated after our competition then had to prepare to travel to Gainesville, Florida for the Junior Olympics. I was like a kid in a candy store—traveling throughout the US to compete in a sport I liked. Coach Howard was pleased with our performance at the NSC, but he wanted to make a statement to all the coaches and athletes that the West Valley Eagles Track Club had the best sprinters in the US.

When we arrived in Florida, I couldn't believe how beautiful everything was. We were going to compete on the Florida University track, and that was unbelievable to me. Weeks ago, I was jumping at the California state meet, and now I was traveling the country, competing against the best in my division. Coach Harold Howard, Roger Lipkis, and the other staff made sure we all got checked into our rooms, then they laid out the rules for our time in Florida. The only things on my mind were competing and meeting girls. I was hoping to meet a nice girl who was as athletic and driven as I was. A couple of athletes from other teams violated the rules and were sent back home. I couldn't believe that an athlete could train so hard, earn their right to be at the Junior Olympics, then do something stupid, and get sent home. Coach Howard and the other assistant coaches surprised us with new uniforms that were unreal. They were bodysuits in red, yellow, blue, and pink with different numbers all over the material. If you didn't know before who the West Valley Eagles were, you were certainly going to know during race day! Our colors were so bright, and the material stuck to our skin like glue.

I was nervous, but I didn't feel anyone could beat us in the relays. We drove to the stadium, went over to the warm-up area, and did our normal warm-up routine. We all felt good, looked good, and had our game faces on. No one could see our new uniforms yet because we all had our shirts covering our bodysuits. We put on our spikes and did some sprints to "feel" the track and get comfortable with our spikes. Once the starter blew the whistle, and we took off our shirts, the stadium went crazy when they saw our uniforms. They were as bright as the sun. Our team knew once we got in the lead, everyone would know who we were.

Sure enough, we devoured our competition and won the 4X100m relay. Our hand-offs were perfect, and it seemed everything ran like a well-oiled machine. We came back and did the same thing in the 4X400m relay, dominating our competition, and running the fastest time in the nation. We got so many compliments about our uniforms but also lots of questions about why we wore such bright colors. I didn't care what we ran in—as long as we won. After the race, I felt as if I were living a dream, with all the good things happening in my life. I wished my mom and sisters could see me run on a national level, but I knew my mom was with me in spirit, guiding every step I took.

The next day, the coaches dropped a huge surprise on us. They took us to Walt Disney World! I lived an hour from Disneyland, in California, but never went because my mom couldn't afford it. Now, here I am in another state—going to Walt Disney World for free! I was very thankful, and it seemed surreal that a poor boy like me was getting the chance to experience the same excitement as people with money. I had a great time that day! I thanked my coaches and couldn't stop thinking about how my summer turned out to be one of the best summers I ever had. I also reflected on how much I had been through. Being in and out of the hospital due to my asthma, having to leave my mom and sisters, and having my track shoes stolen right before my race. Now, I was on top of the world! I learned; it's not how you start but how you finish.

I was ready to get back to California because football was starting soon, and this would be my final season playing high school football. On the plane ride home, we had a little scare. The plane started smoking, and the oxygen masks dropped. Though I was scared, my good friend and teammate, Bryan Howard, got up and jokingly yelled, "We're going to die!" We laughed, but it was a serious matter. I was inexperienced in air travel, so I couldn't take the suspense. Thank God, we arrived back safely to our destination.

Chapter 7

Senior Year

Our football squad was a good deal smaller my senior year, but we still had several talented athletes coming back on offense and defense. I knew DeAndre, Mike M., Matt, Bryan, Mike P., and many others were going to give it all they had and put up a fight, so we could win league. Our crosstown rivals, Norte Vista High and Bloomington High, gave us tough games, but if we all played together and minimized our mistakes, we would be victorious against both teams.

Around this time, I was receiving lots of letters and calls from college recruiters, and I had to decide at the end of the season where I would play college football. I would get very frustrated, at times, talking with college scouts because I was overwhelmed with the process and had a difficult time choosing the right school. There were many times I would go to my room in tears because I didn't know exactly what to say to the scouts when they called. Sometimes, I, purposely, would not answer the phone, and Debbie would say, "Ty, you have to talk to them. I'm not going to make up an excuse for you." It was a great feeling to be wanted and a great problem to have, but I just didn't know where I wanted to play college football. Patrick Johnson, who was heading to Oregon his freshman year, talked to me a lot about going to Oregon. I loved what they had to offer. Don Pellum, who was the scout for Oregon, was my main contact, and I really liked him. He never pressured me and offered me a recruiting trip when my season was over. Debbie and Dan helped me to vet and narrow down the schools, but ultimately, the decision was going to be mine.

I wondered how my mom was doing. I tried to contact her, but I found out from my friend, Mike, who lived in the Heritage Apartments with my mom and sisters, they had moved. I was devasted, and I couldn't believe this crazy man, this abuser, moved my mom and sisters away. Mike did not know where they had moved. I was sad, because even though I wasn't living with my mom and sisters anymore, I could still go by and check on them when he wasn't around. I had a lot on my plate my senior year of high school. I had to focus on school and finish strong, so I could get my life better to, ultimately, help my mom and sisters.

Senior year was comparatively smooth sailing. I only had four periods. I worked hard for three years to pass all my difficult classes, so I could graduate and be eligible to play college sports. The one thing I was worried about was passing my SAT and ACT exams. I wasn't good at taking tests because I would overanalyze everything. But, since Coach Berry's daughter had been tutoring me, I had more confidence in passing the tests.

School started the first week of September, and it seemed like game night came faster than we thought. During the pep rally, we wore our jerseys. I always wore number twenty-five because that's the day my mom was born. Our pregame regimen was always the same. We went to Dairy Queen, and I ordered a Butterfinger Blizzard. We had our team meal, and then I would go to the locker room to get my ankles and wrists taped for the game. We lost our first game, and it seemed our season was going to be one of the worst seasons I had at La Sierra. Every week, when it seemed we would come away with a win, we lost in the closing minutes of the fourth quarter. You could see the frustration on the coaches' and the players' faces.

I did my best to keep our team in the game. I was putting up the numbers on offense and making my hits and tackles on defense, but it wasn't enough. We did win one game, and that gave us some hope, but we had a big game coming up against our crosstown rivals, Notre Vista. There was always lots of trash-talking when we played Notre Vista. I knew most of their players because I played Pop Warner football with them. I heard rumors they wanted to knock me out of the game, but I knew no one on their team could match up with me. They had a fast and shifty quarterback, Matt, and a huge offensive tackle, David. Coach Moore asked me if I would play defensive end to contain Matt, and I gladly accepted. I knew David was 6'5" and about 280 pounds. I was going to make sure I got a quick first step to get to Matt as soon as the ball was snapped. We practiced it all week, and not one of our offensive tackles could stop me.

We played Notre Vista at Riverside Community College, and the day of the game, I was so pumped. It was great seeing many of my former teammates on the field during pregame, but I knew once the referee blew the whistle for the kickoff, it wasn't about friendship anymore. Once pregame was over, my team went back to the locker room to hear Coach Moore give his speech. We all knew how important this victory was—it was about bragging rights. The referee blew the whistle for the captains to come out, so I went with the other captains to the middle of the field for the coin toss. We won the toss, and we deferred to get the ball the second half. We kicked off, and Novi had decent field position. I ran out on the field and lined up as a defensive end, right on the outside of David. Matt lined up under center. He started giving his commands, and I was watching both the ball and David. The center hiked the ball. I flew past David, and Matt barely got the ball off. All night, I pressed Matt hard and ended up sacking him three times. When all was said and done, we ended up losing our last home game to our crosstown rival.

I had many highs and lows during the football season my senior year, but the game that stood out to me the most, during the season, was our game against Bloomington High School. I had seven receptions for 176 yards and a touchdown against the all-mighty Bloomington High. Bloomington had a massive running back, Cheyenne, who would bulldoze over his opponents and flat out intimidate them. I wasn't scared of him and was looking forward to putting a big hit on him. I got my chance when the Bloomington quarterback handed the ball to Cheyenne, and he went straight up the middle. I was on the other side of the field, and I just watched him trample our defense one by one. According to all the players and coaches watching, his touchdown was inevitable until I ran after him like a cheetah stalking its prey and stopped him on the one-yard line. Cheyenne had a thirty or forty-yard lead on me from taking the handoff on his side of the field. I remember when I stopped him on the one-yard line, he asked me why I didn't just let him score, and I said, "Not on my watch." He scored the next play, but I wanted every coach, player, and college scout to see, I was one of the best defensive backs and wide receivers in the state of California. By this time, I had narrowed my recruiting trips to the University of California, Berkeley, the University of Oregon, the University of Purdue, and the University of Colorado.

At the end of the football season, I scheduled my recruiting trips. On recruiting trips to each of these universities, they treated me and the other recruits like royalty. They picked us up from the airport, lavished us with good food, put us in fancy hotels, and connected us with other famous players and alumni. The colleges did everything in their power to convince us to sign with their schools, and they spared no expense doing so. My focus was on the facilities, the food, the parties, and the girls! I got drunk one too many times during these recruiting trips, but I was always able to bounce back the next day and put on a good front, so no one was fully exposed to my wild side.

Out of all the schools, the University of Colorado was probably the school that contacted me the most. They went well out of their way to try to recruit me. They even picked me up in a private jet and gave me total VIP treatment during the process! It was hard saying no to them. On my final recruiting trip, though, I visited the University of Oregon, and that's when everything became real.

I was extremely excited about the trip because I was going to get a chance to see my good friend, Patrick, who was playing at Oregon, as a true freshman. It's extremely hard to play football, as a true freshman, because most student athletes coming out of high school aren't mature enough to handle the demands of learning the team playbook and outdoing veteran players in order to earn a starting position. Don aka "DP" Pellum, who was the linebacker coach for the University of Oregon, made sure Pat was my host, and that I'd get a chance to see the dorms, football facility, Hayward Field, and Autzen Stadium. Pat had already talked to me about U of O while we were running summer track, so I already knew something about the university and life there as a student athlete. When I finally arrived in Oregon, I loved how everything was so green. It reminded me of Woodstock and the free-love movement, and that was appealing to me. Eugene, OR seemed very relaxed and homey, and it made me feel like I was at home.

While I had some alone time in my hotel, I wondered, "How will *this* recruiting trip go?" Because, the other trips I went on were mostly the same. This trip was going in a similar fashion to the others, but on this trip, I met a very gorgeous girl, and we hit it off instantly. We ended up having a lengthy conversation, and I asked her if I could stay in touch with her. She said, "Yes." She told me that when I came back, she would be waiting for me. That made me feel really good.

When I arrived on campus, I fell in love. Oregon made me feel free, and most of the people I encountered were friendly and down-to-earth. On campus, I was able to visit the athletic facilities, the weight room, Hayward Field, and the academic buildings where students attended class. After my tour, I was told there was a special surprise waiting for me at Autzen Stadium later that evening. I couldn't wait to see what else they had up their sleeves! Later that evening, Coach DP took me to the middle of Autzen Stadium on the fifty-yard line. It was dark, and then suddenly, all the lights in the stadium came on. An announcer over the intercom said, "Ladies and gentlemen, I want to introduce you to the starting cornerback, number 25, 5'10," and weighing in at 160 pounds, from Riverside, La Sierra High—Tyree Washington! I looked up, and everyone was wearing an Oregon Ducks' jersey with my last name and number on the back. I was speechless. I couldn't believe how badly the Oregon Ducks wanted me. DP took me up into the sky box where they had a special dinner for me. My jersey was front and center, so I could see what I would be wearing, as a true freshman, playing football at the University of Oregon. I was sold. I knew right then and there I was going to sign my letter of intent to the University of Oregon.

When I got back home, I told Dan and Debbie, Coach Berry, and Coach Moore I was going to sign with the University of Oregon to play football. Everyone was happy, but it was bittersweet because I couldn't share the news with my mom. She moved to an unknown place. I tried to maintain my focus and constantly give myself pep talks that I was doing the right thing. Once my life got better, the rest of my family's lives would, too. 1994 was coming to a close and within a couple of months, I would be letting the country know who I would be playing football for in the fall of 1995.

I had a great time spending Christmas with the Passalacqua family, but I always thought of my mom and sisters. I missed them so much. I missed the long talks with my sister Rosalyn, because she was my best friend and road dog. I missed lying on the sofa with my mom and laying my head on her shoulder. I was her only boy, and I was her baby. She would do anything for me, and it was that way my whole life. What eased the pain of not being with my family was that I was going to college to make something of my life. Her boyfriend couldn't do anything about it. He wanted me to fail, but I had a solid support system with Dan, Debbie, Coach Moore, and Coach Berry. They were not going to let me fail, and I loved every one of them for making a sacrifice to help me accomplish my dream.

The next two months went by fast, and on February 1, 1995, I signed my letter of intent to play Division 1 football at the University of Oregon. I was happy that after four football seasons of wondering if I would get a football scholarship, my dream came true. I had overcome leaving home at sixteen, battling asthma, and struggling with my eating disorder, to receive a football scholarship. I was named all-state for medium schools, and that was a huge accomplishment. In my mind, I was the best cornerback in the state of California. My last year of track was right around the corner, and I wanted to go out with a bang. Coach Berry and I made it clear that my goal was to repeat as state champion in the long jump and then win state in the 400m. But, in the middle of my senior year, I met a beautiful distraction.

A beautiful girl moved from Barstow to attend La Sierra. She was extremely attractive, with a body like a model. After a short time knowing her, she agreed to be my girlfriend, to my coaches and my counselors dismay. They didn't want this relationship to be a distraction, and they knew the likelihood of us staying in a relationship, since I was going off to Oregon, and she'd remain at the school, was slim. I, though, was careful to maintain my grades and my focus on my final track season.

I dominated every league and invitational meet I competed in. Although my main goal was football, I really wanted to leave high school as the state champion in the long jump and 400m. As expected, I won league in the 400m, made it to CIF, and dominated my competition to earn a trip to the state championships.

My girlfriend was very proud of me, and she had her own dreams. She was taking drama at school, and her goals were to become a model and actress. She would recite her lines to me, and I was amazed at how she could remember all that information. I saw us as being a couple—maybe even getting married one day. Dan and Debbie were doing their best to help keep me focused on the main goal—the University of Oregon. I needed to finish out my track season, pass my SAT or ACT, and graduate from high school. But, I was so in love, my relationship was clouding my judgement.

I made it to state again in the 400m. I was right back at Cerritos Community College, gearing up for an epic battle against Obea Moore, a runner from Pasadena. When we arrived at the stadium, it seemed like more people than ever had packed themselves in the stadium to watch me compete against him. Some people had a picture of Obea on their shirts—I couldn't believe it! You couldn't miss Obea because he had a big afro. Girls and adults would flock to be near him and watch him run. He was already a rock star in high school. I didn't care about all the excitement about Obea. I wanted to slay him like David slew Goliath.

Since my track shoes had been stolen the previous year, this time Coach Berry held my shoes in his arms. He made sure no one would get to them. I stood in the stands with my coaches, watching the relays and other events, but soon it was time to go warm up. I felt good in the warm-up area, and I couldn't wait to get on the track and battle Obea. Obea was going to be in the lane inside of me, so I knew I had to do my best to get out fast. The starter blew the whistle to get ready. I stood behind my starting blocks with my heart pumping like pistons in a car. The starter said, "Runners, take your mark, (I took a deep breath) set, go."

I took off and was feeling good. I heard the crowd getting louder and louder. Obea must be picking up the pace. He caught up to me fast, and then I picked it up. We came around the second turn, and Obea had a slight lead, but I kept telling myself, "You're strong, and you will be able to snatch him up." As we're on the last straight-away, Obea was winning, and I needed to pick it up *quickly*. I started gaining ground on him, but right when I felt like I was going to nip him at the tape, he crossed the finish line before me. I was disappointed but congratulated him and the other runners. Then, we all received our medals on the podium.

I hated the fact I lost. I kept replaying the race over in my head, as athletes always do. If I would have gotten out harder and picked it up on the second turn, it would have given me a lead, and Obea wouldn't have been able to beat me. I walked to my coaches, and they congratulated me for a job well done. I had a great track career, and I kept telling myself, "You have nothing to be ashamed of." My girlfriend was immensely proud of me.

I started having the desire to be closer to my girlfriend, so I, eventually, told Dan and Debbie I was going to move in with her. Naturally, they were totally against it because they knew it wasn't a good move for me at this time in my life. I ended up making the decision based on my feelings instead of what was right for my future.

My last SAT test was scheduled. I passed all my core classes and met the requirements for the NCAA. Mike and DeAndre, two of my best friends, were excited for me because I was going to play Division 1 football. It was hard to leave them behind because we spent so much time together playing video games, talking about girls, playing golf, and being at each other's houses.

The day of my graduation from La Sierra High School, in Riverside, California, June 15, 1995, I was dressed up – wearing a tie! Mike and DeAndre were looking good, too. Mike's mom, Annette and Mundo were there as were Dan and Debbie. My girlfriend was there, too. I had to wait a long time to get my diploma because they went by alphabetical order. I wished my mom and sisters could have been there to witness something only a few people in my family had accomplished. I knew, even though my mom wasn't there, she was praying for me daily and smiling, knowing I had made it.

I took the final SAT that was scheduled, and about a month later, my results came in. I didn't pass. I was so devasted because I wanted to play football at the University of Oregon. I had bags and bags of letters from colleges all around the country who wanted me. I threw them all in the trash. I felt like a failure. I couldn't believe that one test would prevent me from playing college football and living my dream. I called Coach Moore and Coach Berry to tell them the bad news. They notified Don Pellum and told him what had happened. Don Pellum told me not to worry because the NCAA had a new rule that any incoming student athlete who failed to meet the qualifications to receive a NCAA athletic scholarship could benefit from Prop 48. This enabled me to sit out one year, attend community college, and attend classes at the university the next fall.

Riverside Rams. (Courtesy of Ms. Williams)   Riverside Steelers. (Courtesy of Ms. Williams)

My childhood friend, Robert Grizzle and I taking a photo near his apartment in the late 1980's. (Courtesy of Robert Grizzle)

On the steps at my best friend's house Robert Grizzle in the late 1980's. (Courtesy of Robert Grizzle)

Hanging out with my sister at her home in Riverside, California. (Courtesy of Joyce Davis)

Running down Ramiah Jackson before he tried to score another touchdown during the 1994 high school football season. (Courtesy of Ramiah Jackson)

Looking down field to try and score another La Sierra touchdown during the 1994 High School Football Season. (Courtesy of La Sierra High School Yearbook)

Competing at the 1995 Riverside Track and Field Invitational at the University of California Riverside. (Courtesy of La Sierra High School Yearbook)

1995 La Sierra High School graduation with me, my best friend Mike and his little brother Mundo. (Courtesy of Annette Gomez)

Working out with the speed chute at San Bernardino Valley College during my 1997 Track and Field season. (Courtesy of Blackman Ihem)

My Junior College Coach Blackman Ihem gave me some coaching advice after my workout at San Bernardino Valley College in 1997. (Courtesy of Blackman Ihem)

Competing for San Bernardino Valley College in 1997 while wearing my trademark headband. (Courtesy of Kenneth Blumenthal)

My first apartment in Chino Hills, California 1998. (Courtesy of Tyree Washington)

Hugging Winslow Garnier after getting baptized in 1999 while Jim Fulcher cheers for me. (Courtesy of Tyree Washington)

My two NFL agents Doc and JJ made my dream become a reality when the San Diego Chargers signed me in 1999. (Courtesy of JJ Flournoy)

Tyree Washington
Wide Receiver

1999 San Diego Chargers photo. (Courtesy of Los Angeles Chargers)

Signing my contract so JJ Flournoy can represent me as my NFL agent. (Courtesy of JJ Flournoy)

Paying my respect in New York to the victims who lost their lives in 911. (Courtesy of Tyree Washington)

Monica and I in Minnesota on vacation. (Courtesy of Tyree Washington)

Me and Monica taking a quick selfie in our taxi before we go to dinner. (Courtesy of Tyree Washington)

Coach Blackman Ihem aka "Pops" always encouraged me to strive for greatness and to never settle for anything else. (Courtesy of Blackman Ihem)

Taking some time to hang out with my former training partner Christopher Williams and Coach Blackman Ihem. (Courtesy of Tyree Washington)

Hall of Fame track & field coach Jim Bush always taught me to be a student of the game. (Courtesy of Monica Washington)

My eldest son Malik and I at his high school graduation. (Courtesy of Tyree Washington)

Receiving my 2003 World Championship Gold Medal from former CEO of USATF Doug Logan. (Courtesy of Kirby Lee)

4X400 Relay Award Ceremony at the 2003 Outdoor World Championships in Saint-Denis, France. (Courtesy of Kirby Lee)

In complete shock I took second at the 2003 Outdoor World Championships in Saint-Denis, France in the 400m. (Courtesy of Kirby Lee)

Letting the world know I'm back. (Courtesy of Kirby Lee)

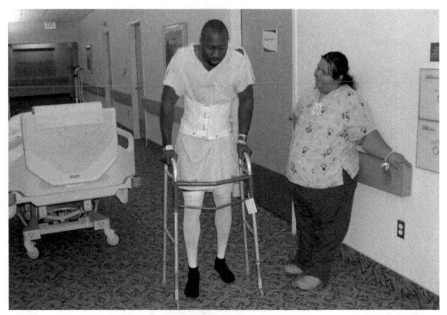

Doing rehab at Saint John Hospital in Los Angeles, California after my back surgery in 2007. (Courtesy of Tyree Washington)

2013 Riverside Sports Hall of Fame Induction in my hometown. (Courtesy of Tyree Washington)

Life may be tough, but I keep smiling. (Courtesy of Mundo Gomez)

Supporting Monica at her promotion to become a Sergeant in the Army. (Courtesy of Monica Washington)

Happy times with my former Head Track and Field Coach Kenneth Blumenthal at my 2017 San Bernardino Valley College Hall of Fame Induction. (Courtesy of Tyra Washington)

Me, my former high school football coach and his wife Cami at my 2017 Hall of Fame Induction at San Bernardino Valley College. (Courtesy of Tyra Washington)

When I was in high school, God sent me two angels, Dan and Debbie Passalacqua to become my surrogate parents. (Courtesy of Debbie Passalacqua)

Family photo with Monica and our kids. (Courtesy of Monica Washington)

2005 Underwater photo shoot. (Courtesy of Howard Schatz)

Chapter 8

Instability

I spent four years in high school, giving it my all in the classroom to get good grades, performing on the football field to impress each and every football recruiter who came out to see me, and all I had to do was get a passing score on my SAT, and I was home free. My dream soon became a nightmare, and my smooth path became a rocky road. I went into damage control to try and figure out how I could turn my bad situation into something good. That's when I received a new chance at life to attend the University of Oregon to play football.

Don Pellum arranged for me to leave for Eugene, Oregon and enroll at Lane Community College in the fall. He also arranged for me to stay with Patrick for a while; eventually, I would get my own place. Before leaving, I had the opportunity to see my girlfriend perform in a beauty pageant, and it gave me an opportunity to see her in her element—beautifully adorned in pageant attire, looking like a cover model on Vogue magazine. My girlfriend was heavily involved in beauty pageants and competed across many cities and states. When it came time to say goodbye to her and fly to Oregon, it was not an easy decision. Although, we were both sad about the separation, I explained to her this was my dream, and if I wanted to make something of myself and help us to have a secure future, I needed to go to college. My goal was to get my degree in psychology, play three years at U of O, and then go to the NFL.

When I arrived in Eugene, OR, I felt like things were starting to come together. I was one step closer to my dream. Living with Pat was a gift. I was able to work out regularly and get ready for school in the fall. Back home, my girlfriend was missing me a great deal. Little did I know, both of our lives were getting ready to dramatically change. One day, my girlfriend called and said, "I have news to give you." I thought maybe she got a deal for a commercial, an acting job, or won a major beauty pageant. As I sat in suspense over the phone, she said, "I'm pregnant."

I, immediately, felt as if someone punched me in the stomach and knocked the wind out of me. I was thinking, "How could this happen?" But, I *knew* how it happened. One day, we were careless and slipped up. My girlfriend was scared and very fearful to tell her mom because having a baby would put a hold on her modeling and acting career. I couldn't help but think we were too young to have a baby, but we had to deal with the consequences of our actions. Though it was a hard pill to swallow, I knew, if I helped to make this baby, I was going to have to be a man and take care of it.

I told Pat and, eventually, shared the news with Don. He was so encouraging and uplifting and said everything would work out. He said I needed to remain in Oregon to start school in the fall, and the following year I would be at U of O playing football. Don also told me he could help me and my girlfriend get an apartment, while I attended school at Lane Community College. I called my girlfriend and told her that Don would help us get an apartment, and she could get a job and go to the junior college, also. She seemed very reluctant to leave her mother in California. I told her it would be a great opportunity for us to be together, and we could raise our child in Eugene, while I pursued my dream to play college football that would eventually lead to a better life for us all.

She finally mustered enough courage to tell her mom she was pregnant. To put it lightly, her mother did not take it well, and my girlfriend told me she was not coming with me. My heart was broken. I pleaded with her, but she was firm in her decision. So, I told Don I was going back home to help my girlfriend with the baby. Both Don and Pat were against my decision, but all I could think about was not having a father in my life. I didn't want my child to experience growing up without a father.

Back home in California, I couldn't move back in with my girlfriend because her mom was furious I got her daughter pregnant. I went to live with my best friend, Mike, at his parents' house in Riverside. I didn't have a job, money, or a car. Mike's parents were like a mother and a father to me. They helped me with food, clothes, transportation, and money.

I decided to enroll at Riverside Community College (RCC) in the fall of 1995 to play football. It seemed most of my high school teammates and friends from other high schools were playing for RCC. Coach Maier was the head coach. I heard he was tough, but he was good at helping players get into a four-year university. We had a great squad. Some who came from my high school team were Sammy, Brad, Mike, and Mickey (the state champion in the 300m hurdles in high school).

By this time, it's obvious I'm not in Oregon, which led to several people asking me why I was in Riverside and not at the University of Oregon. I told them it didn't work out because I didn't pass my SAT and ACT. Most athletes on the football team were playing for RCC because they had academic or behavioral issues—or they had gone to a major college but couldn't handle the demands of being a student athlete.

I was nervous to play college ball because I was small, and a large number of the players on the team were huge. I was the fastest on the team, but I didn't know if I could take a hit from players that significantly outweighed me. One of the games we played was against Long Beach City College. During the game, I had over a hundred yards rushing on special teams. I was maneuvering through players on the field like I was playing dodgeball. Long Beach players were huge, but they couldn't handle my speed. After about four games at RCC, I left because the head coach and I weren't on the same page.

I was back at square one. Out of school with a baby on the way and no clue about my next steps. At this point, I'm thinking my athletic career is over, and I need to get a full-time job to support my child. One day, I meet Coach Blackman Ihem in Riverside, and he tells me he's been following my athletic career in track, since I was in high school. He knew all my running stats, and he told me if I gave him one year to coach me, he would make me into a world-class track and field athlete. I looked at him, laughed, and replied, "Everyone says they can make me great!" He assured me I could be one of the best 400m runners in history. I told him I was trying to get back to a four-year college, so I could play football and then go to the NFL. That was my focus. That was my dream. He told me if things didn't work out, then I should call him.

It had been almost two years since the last time I saw my mom. She still lived with her abusive boyfriend, so I talked to my best friends, Gabe and Shawndale, to help me come up with a plan to get my mom and sisters away from him. They were living in a small house on the eastside of Riverside. I called and told my mother and sisters about the plan my friends and I came up with. They had grown weary of the abuse and agreed with the plan. The plan was once I got to their house, I was going to knock on the door and tell my mom's boyfriend I was sorry for all I had done and ask him to accept me back. Then, I would distract him, while my mom and sisters ran out the door and got into the car with Gabe and Shawndale.

The day finally came to execute the plan. I was extremely nervous, but I knew Gabe and Shawndale would have my back if it went sour. We drove to my mom's house, and just like we planned, I went to the door. My mom's boyfriend answered, and I told him I was sorry for what I did and asked him to accept me back. He asked me if I was sorry, and I said, "Yes." So, he hugged me (which was awkward), and then we walked in the house. He yelled for my mom and sisters to come greet me, and they did. After talking to my mom and sisters for a while, he went back in the room to get something, and I told my mom and sisters to run out the door to the car. Once he heard the door slam, he started yelling my mom's name, "Mattie, Mattie!" He said, "Where did they go? You tricked me!" He went to grab his gun, and I ran out the door, jumped in the car, and we were gone. He yelled, screamed, and accused me of kidnapping.

He ended up reporting me to the police, but we had already reached the police station to tell them my mom wanted to leave him, but he wouldn't let her. The officer told him my mom left of her own free will, which made him even more irate. We decided to take my mom to file a restraining order against him. When her court date came, the judge asked my mother whether she wanted to leave her boyfriend, and she said, "Yes." "Did anyone force you to leave against your will?" he asked. My mom said, "No."

I was proud of my mom for speaking up and telling the judge she had been abused and didn't want to be with her boyfriend anymore. Her boyfriend was mad. He spoke out of order and said I kidnapped my mom. The judge looked and him and said, "Did you hear what she had to say? She doesn't want you anymore." He told my mom's boyfriend he needed to be at least one-hundred feet away from my mother, or he'd be arrested.

I was relieved and filled with joy that finally my mother and sisters were back with me, after not seeing them for over a year. My mom and sisters went to live with Aunt Betty for a while until they got their own apartment. My sister Rosalyn started attending Job Corps in San Bernardino where she met a guy named Steven, who, eventually, became her boyfriend. Steven was set to start art school in San Francisco. Because Rosalyn wanted to be with him, she dropped out of Job Corps and moved to San Francisco. Eventually, we all moved to San Francisco—my mom, my other sister, me, and my girlfriend. We wanted a change of scene, and so five months into my girlfriend's pregnancy, we moved to San Francisco to live with Rosalyn and her boyfriend.

To our dismay, when we arrived in San Francisco, we discovered my sister and her boyfriend were living in a hotel in what seemed to be a basement, with no extra room for all of us! The thought of having my pregnant girlfriend living under these conditions was upsetting.

All throughout this time, my mind was still focused on my goal of playing college football. My agenda in San Francisco was to enroll at Merritt Junior College in East Oakland, so I could compete in track and field, get my AA degree, and transfer to a four-year school. Maurice Compton was courting me to attend Merritt College because he said under his guidance, I could become a world-class track and field athlete. I bought into what he was saying because I had nothing to lose and everything to gain. I had a baby on the way, no money, and no job, so I needed to get my life together ASAP.

To get to Merritt College, I had to take the BART train from San Francisco. It was my first time taking the subway. It was also my first time going to East Oakland, which I heard was rough, and I would need to have my head on a swivel. I grew up in a rough neighborhood, but this was new terrain for me. Back home, I knew most of the people on my block.

Going back and forth to Oakland was hard financially. I had little money, my girlfriend wasn't eating the way she should, and between us, we only had one bag of clothes. I'm not a quitter but staying in San Francisco was turning out to be a bad idea. It wasn't planned out properly, and my sister and her boyfriend lied about their housing accommodations. To make things worse, when my girlfriend called her mom and told her she had run off with me to San Francisco, her mom told her if she didn't come home, she would call the police and have them bring her home. I called Coach Compton and told him, "My girlfriend needs to go back home because her mom is threatening to call the police because she ran away." He asked me what I was going to do. I said, "I think it's best if we go back home." He wanted me to stay and attend school at Merritt, but I couldn't leave the mother of my child to deal with this pregnancy on her own. I helped create the baby, so I needed to be responsible and be right by her side when she needed me. My girlfriend left San Francisco first, and then my mom, sister, and I decided it wasn't the place for us to be either, so we all left.

My mom and sister were able to get an apartment in Riverside through the housing department, which was great. They had been held captive for years, but slowly and surely, they were getting back on their feet to living a life of freedom. I moved back in with my best friend, Mike, and his family.

When my girlfriend returned home, she received plenty of backlash from her family and friends. She became extremely overwhelmed and didn't want to talk to me much. I was devastated. One day, she called and asked if I could bring her some Chinese food.

I was a ten-minute drive away, but since I didn't have a car, I rode a bike to her house to give her the Chinese food. When I dropped off her food, my heart raced, and I felt badly we weren't together. She visited with me for a while, but I couldn't stay long because if her mother saw her with me, she would be truly angry. I rode all the way back to Mike's house, crying and frustrated that our relationship might be coming to an end.

Weeks passed by, and we hardly communicated at all. She called me, one day, and said she was going to stay with her sister, for a while, in another city about an hour and a half away, to clear her head. She said once she was ready to talk about our relationship, she would let me know. My mind was spinning out of control with negative thoughts. "Maybe, she met someone else who she wanted to be in the baby's life."

She didn't call me for days. I was afraid she was cutting me out of her life, and I wanted to tell her how much I loved and cared for her and our baby, so I borrowed money from Mike to buy a Greyhound ticket. I bought a one-way Greyhound ticket, and Mike thought I was losing my mind. When I arrived, it was late in the evening, and I was hungry and cold. I walked over to her sister's apartment to make sure she was still in the same place, and I kept wondering what I was going to say to my girlfriend when I saw her the following day.

"What if she tells me she doesn't want anything to do with me or yells at me for coming to see her?" I thought to myself. I didn't know what to expect. All I knew was she was the woman I loved, and I needed to do anything I could to win her back. It was getting late, and I didn't have any money for a hotel, nor did I know anyone in the town. I found an unlocked building complex and slept in the corner on the floor by an empty office, using my jacket as a blanket. I was scared I would get mugged, killed, or bitten by a wild animal, but I took the risk, just so I could talk to my girlfriend. I slept with one eye open, and it seemed the night lasted forever.

The next morning, I got up dirty, hungry, and desperate to speak with my girlfriend. I gathered up the courage to walk over to her sister's apartment. It took all the strength in me to ball up my fist to knock on the door. She was shocked and couldn't believe I had come all that way just to see her. She asked who I stayed with, and I told her I slept outside all night in an abandoned building complex. She said I was crazy, and she was right—I was crazy in love with her and our baby. I told her how much I loved her, and I was sorry about taking her to San Francisco.

She said she didn't know if it was going to work out between us. She wasn't sure her mom would accept me back. I was crushed but was savoring the moment of just being there with her. Luckily, she and her sister were planning to drive back to town that day and offered me a ride. On the drive back, we spoke very little. She dropped me off at Mike's house and went back to her house. Now, I was more confused than before and totally unclear about the future of our relationship.

While things were not going so well between my girlfriend and I, as fate would have it, I met a gentleman whose son went to my high school. He told me if I still wanted to play college ball at the Division 1 level, I could. I was extremely interested, but I didn't know if he was being sincere. He told me he could get me and another one of my high school teammates into Jackson State, which was in Mississippi, to play football. He said he needed my transcripts, SAT and ACT scores, and any documentation that I had registered with the NCAA Clearing-house. I told him I had completed all the admissions' requirements and had signed with the University of Oregon but failed to meet the SAT requirements, leaving me to sit out a year. He told me as long as I didn't use up my first year of freshman eligibility to play football, I could enroll at Jackson State. I was so happy, but at the same time, nervous to tell my girlfriend. We weren't on good terms, and her mom was mad at me. I needed to step up and be a man to show that I could take care of my baby.

Weeks passed. I got a call from the gentleman, who told me and my high school teammate, we were accepted to attend Jackson State, and we would need to get there right away. We had to leave the very next day via Greyhound, no less! When I told my girlfriend I was leaving, she was extremely upset. I told her once again, I needed to leave to get my life back to take care of her and the baby. She was hurt, but I felt I had no other choice. I didn't want to waste the talent

God gave me just because I was scared to make a move into the unknown.

We got on the Greyhound the next morning and were on our way to Mississippi. It was January of 1996. We both knew it was going to be an awfully long bus ride to Jackson State. As we traveled the country, I slept mostly and thought about my future. I thought, "When am I going to get a big break?" My efforts to attend the University of Oregon failed because I didn't meet the SAT requirements. I played four games at Riverside Community College, and that didn't last. Now, I was off to Jackson State, wondering if this would last. My thoughts were all over the place, and I was very anxious. I believe, my friend, sitting next to me, felt the same way. We had some good conversations about our dreams on the bus ride, but we didn't quite know what was going to happen once we arrived in Mississippi.

When we got to Mississippi, I felt like I was in the old west. Things seemed terribly slow. It was cold and gloomy, and perhaps it was my paranoia, but it seemed as if people knew we were from out of state. When we arrived at the dorms, the people at the desk said we weren't in the system. I couldn't believe we traveled all the way from California to Mississippi just to find out we're not in the system. We called the gentleman, who allegedly, helped us get into Jackson State, and he said he would work it out. We were concerned and weren't banking on it and had no money to return home if we wanted to.

As the evening wore on, we were told there was nothing they could do for us that night, but they allowed us to stay in the dorms until a resolution was found. I was starting not to like this school. They placed us in an empty room, and there was no hot water or blankets. We couldn't clean ourselves because we had no hygiene products.

The next day, one of the coaches came by to check on us. He said there was an issue with our enrollment, and they would need to sort it out. He said, in the meantime, he would help us with food, blankets, hygiene products, and other things we needed for our room. I was like, "Whatever . . ." at that point. I was already checking out. I kept thinking about my girlfriend and our baby. I figured if I were going to do badly, I could do it in my own city, close to my family and girlfriend.

I called and told my girlfriend, "It was a mistake coming down here, so I'm going to come back home as soon as I find a way." My friend wanted me to stay and stick it out and so did the coaches and the gentleman who paid for me to go out to Mississippi, but I was done. I called my mom and asked if she could buy me a bus ticket to come home, and she said, "Yes." I, quietly, departed for California—avoiding my friend who I knew was upset with me.

I spent a good deal of time crying on the Greyhound bus back home, thinking about how I was a loser because I couldn't get into college to play football. After three long days of crying, barely eating, and sleeping most of the time, I arrived in San Bernardino. I called Coach Blackman Ihem, the assistant track coach at San Bernardino Valley College, who once told me if football didn't work out, to give him a call because he could help me become one of the greatest 400m runners ever.

Just as promised, he picked me up at the Greyhound bus station and took me to get something to eat. While we were eating, I told him I had a baby on the way, and I had no place to stay, no job, and no money. He told me he'd help me get back on my feet, and that if I believed in him, I would become one of the greatest sprinters ever. I felt broken and desperate, but I felt in my gut Coach Blackman was sincere about making me into a great 400m runner.

My girlfriend was extremely happy I was back home. Her mother even allowed me to move back in with them because she felt we needed to be together, since our baby was on the way.

I took Coach Blackman's advice and enrolled at San Bernardino Valley College in the winter of 1996, just so I could become eligible to run for the San Bernardino Valley track team in the 1997 spring track season. I made a commitment to myself and coach Blackman to train with his track club, New Era, in the winter and spring of 1996, hoping to make the Olympic team. I knew my schedule would be challenging, since I was taking college courses at San Bernardino Valley. I was training with the New Era track team, and I needed to support my girlfriend because we had a baby on the way. Getting back and forth to school was a struggle. Sometimes, I got a ride from Coach Blackman or one of the hurdlers on the track team, but sometimes I would miss class. The days that I missed class, I was taking my girlfriend to her doctor's appointments, training for track on a dirt hill by her house, and looking for a job.

I was very worried about how I was going to support my son when I didn't have a job. I was hoping every day I could find a job, but more importantly, I wanted to earn another athletic scholarship, so I could go pro in track and field. I spent my whole life wanting to be in the NFL, but that had to take a back seat, so I could become a world-class track athlete.

Coach Blackman had a great track club with some of the most talented male and female athletes I ever saw. I had the pleasure to train with high school phenom, Theodosia Russell, who ran the 400m, and sprint sensation, Pete, who ran the 100m. Russell and I would have all-out wars during practice, running repeat 300m, 500m, and anything else Coach Blackman wanted us to do. I had a lot of respect for the New Era athletes because I knew we would make each other better. My goal was to qualify for the Olympic Trials in the 400m, but I had to start from the bottom and work my way up to the top.

From day one, Coach Blackman told me that I was a professional athlete. I looked at him confused, and then he explained, even though I wasn't a professional athlete right then, I needed to train, eat, think, dress, practice, and compete like one. He said that whether I was competing in college or professionally, he wanted me to be superior and dominate all my opponents. That resonated with me and worked to eliminate my intimidation of other opponents because of the mental and physical training which was preparing me to be on the same level as any world-class track and field runner.

It was almost time for my girlfriend to have our baby boy, and I was feeling the pressure. Pressure to get a job, run fast enough to qualify for the 1996 Olympics, and make sure I passed all my classes at Valley College.

My girlfriend went into labor on April 3, 1996, and on April 4th, she had our baby boy. He was a healthy and handsome young fellow. My girlfriend wanted to name him Malik, after the actor Malik Yoba, but I wanted to name him Blake. After some debate and disagreement, I finally gave in, and he was named Malik. Watching the birth of a child was an amazing experience.

My girlfriend stayed in the hospital for a while because our son had jaundice and colic. When they were finally cleared to be released from the hospital, the doctor instructed us to keep Malik in the sun, so he could get rid of his yellowish skin. At this point, I was still in shock that I was an actual father. My mind was set on being a better father than the one I never knew.

Our first day home with Malik was surreal. We were making formula, changing diapers, listening to him cry at night, and just getting acquainted with this new world. We were fortunate that friends and family bought us clothes, diapers, and other essential things we needed for him. Because neither my girlfriend nor I had a job, she got on welfare to help us get on our feet. It was an awful reminder for me of what it was like being on welfare when I was a little boy. I didn't want that life for my son, so I was determined to do whatever it took to provide for my family.

Eventually, I got a job through my girlfriend's mom's boyfriend at a hypermarket, working on the stocking crew from 11pm to 7am. I knew my schedule was going to be a little challenging because I had school right after work, track in the afternoon, and then I would need to race home, so I could help take care of the baby and get some rest before work.

Malik was able to get over his colic and jaundice, and that was a relief to us. When my girlfriend and I took Malik for a walk, I felt so proud to have a baby who would be an extension of me. God blessed me with the gift to have a son to carry on my name, and I was thankful. I loved my girlfriend deeply. Eventually, I wanted us to get married, have more babies, and live the rest of our lives together.

Chapter 9

Between Two Worlds

In the spring of 1996, I competed at the Mt. Sac Relays in the 400m and won my heat. I ran 46.87, which was a great time for me, since I was hardly training because of my busy schedule. Coach Blackman told me I was right on track to run the speed I needed, in the spring of 1997. I trusted him and believed him. I ran in one last track meet to better my 400m time to 46 flat. That time gave me the Olympic B qualifying standard to compete at the Olympic Trials in Atlanta. I was happy to qualify, but Coach Blackman told me that he preferred I didn't compete at the Olympic Trials because I barely met the qualifying standard. He said if I competed in the Olympic Trials, I would get knocked out the first round. He said if I had a better fall training, there would be no doubt I would make the Olympic team. I agreed with him because I wanted to be at my best when I competed.

The plan was to take the summer off from competing but to put tons of mileage in, three times a week, no weights, and get ready to train hard in the fall of 1996. By 1997, I would break every California junior college record, win the US Outdoor Nationals, beat Michael Johnson, make the World Outdoor Championship team, win the gold medal in the 400m, and be ranked number one in the world. I was ready for the challenge to become one of the greatest 400m runners the world had ever seen.

One day on the job, I was feeling the pressure of how much I was juggling my schedule and decided I would use my break to take a short nap. My manager saw me and didn't realize I was on break. He told me I needed to go home because I was sleeping on the job. I tried to explain to him I was on break, and my co-workers did the same, but he wasn't havin' it. Days later, I received a call from my job and was told I was fired. I was angry and fought back because I needed that job. That was the only source of income I could truly rely on to provide for my family.

My relationship with my girlfriend began to suffer. I would reflect, look at my life, and was appalled by what I saw. A little over a year ago, I was on top of the world—racking up accolades in track and football and signing a full-ride scholarship to the University of Oregon. Now, I was at rock bottom, trying to climb my way back out of the gutter.

My job, eventually, called me weeks after firing me and asked if I wanted my job back. I told them I didn't want to come back and work for them. At this point, I decided I wanted to dedicate my life to becoming a great 400-meter runner. That wasn't going to happen, though, without a consistent training schedule. Coach Blackman told me I needed to move closer to San Bernardino Valley College, so I could be closer to school. I was currently living in Corona, Ca. So, once again, I was on the move.

I told my girlfriend I was moving out, and she was upset and hurt, yelling, and begging me to stay. I couldn't. I knew I needed to make this sacrifice, so I got a garbage bag, threw all my clothes in it, and headed for my mom's house.

It was the summer of 1996. My training plan was in full effect. I made it my priority to do everything Coach Blackman wanted me to do, and even though my girlfriend and I were at odds, I helped take care of my son as much as I could. I waited patiently for Coach Blackman and the head coach of my track team at Valley College, help me get a place to stay which was closer to school. I couldn't wait for the fall because I knew my life was going to change for the better.

I ended up staying with one of my childhood friends, Ricky, who was also on the track team. The plan was for this to be temporary until I could get an apartment with four other teammates. Ricky lived in a two-bedroom apartment with his girlfriend and two other athletes who also ran on the track team. I was super grateful to have a place to lay my head, even though it was on a sofa. Ricky had a job working at Popeye's Chicken, and after work, his boss would let him bring home chicken and biscuits. I was so happy because I had hardly any money and wasn't eating well throughout the day, so Popeye's was a gourmet meal for me! There were many nights I stayed up late, talking to Ricki and my other teammates about breaking track records, going off to college, making the Olympic team, and winning state titles in our events. I dreamed about being the best 400m runner in the world and beating the great Michael Johnson.

I couldn't believe it, but I had been running for two months just as Coach Blackman instructed me to do. Finally, it was time to start the fall semester at Valley College. I had to make sure I took twelve units, so I would be eligible to compete in the spring 1997 track season. Coach Blackman sat me down one day and shared with me the importance of setting goals for my life. He asked me to write down specific goals for my spirituality, family, school, finances, and track. I knew I wanted to win state in the 400m and 200m, break the national record in the 400m and 200m, win the 400m in the Outdoor US Nationals, win the World Outdoor Championships in the 400m, and be the number one 400m runner on earth. Being great and accomplishing these goals was about making sure my son had a life I never had.

Valley College was a unique school. It was in a very tough neighborhood, and most of the students like me were poor, had probably been in jail, were single parents, involved in gangs, drug dealers, and so much more. I felt at home because I grew up in a similar environment. All the drama and hostility didn't bother me at all. I was about my business, and I wanted to get back on top, despite giving up my Division 1 football scholarship to take care of my son. To be preparing like a professional athlete, the environment, and the school, itself, didn't lend to that reality. The track was half cement and half synthetic. The weight room looked like it was made back in the days of the Roman empire. I needed that hard knock environment because it was going to make me tougher, and all my track coaches knew that. They knew where I came from, and that's why they wanted me at Valley College.

My fall training was intense. I trained at the University of California, Riverside, with New Era in the evening and then would go back to Valley College and work out in the weight room. Coach Blackman looked out for me and treated me as if I were his son, always making sure I had everything I needed.

Around this time, I decided to end my relationship with my son's mother. Our lives were headed in different directions, and my main priority was my son. I moved out of Ricky's apartment into my own apartment that I ended up sharing with three other athletes from Valley College. The head coach helped us to secure the apartment. I had no job, but he made it happen!

When we moved into the apartment, I felt like everything was coming together. I had a secure place of my own to live. I was enrolled in school. I had a great sprint coach and a plan to become the number one 400m runner in the world the following year. Even though my roommates and I didn't have much money, we helped each other out with food and found ways to get rides from other athletes who lived in our apartment complex. We were all becoming one big family, and I loved that. We all had the same goal—get our degrees and transfer to another college to play Division 1 sports.

I started to put my goals in motion. I hung them up in my room, in my school folder, and I had an index card with my goals on it in my backpack. I wanted to remind myself every day of the goals I was working to obtain. I trained when my asthma was flaring up, and when it was cold, hot, or windy. I did repeat hills over 300m in Riverside, repeat 400m with the speed chutes on the track, and I'd put in two miles after my workout. There were many times I'd be in my apartment with nothing to do and would go for a late-night run by myself, just to put in more mileage.

I wasn't afraid of anything anymore, and my confidence level was sky high. I was getting world-class training, and I felt the only person who could beat me was me. I finished up my last month of rigorous training, and Coach Blackman found me an all-comers meet to compete in. I went into the competition nervous because I wanted to do well, but Coach assured me that this was another practice—just with new people. Every 800m I ran was going to help me become stronger in the 400m than I had ever been.

Quickly, like before, things took a turn. At Mount San Antonio College, I ran a 800m in two minutes and then decided to run a hundred meters. Everything was fine during my warmup, but in the middle of my race, I felt as if someone shot me in the back, and I dropped to the ground in agony, grasping my hamstring. My mind immediately went to wasted time and another defeat. I instantly thought all I had worked for was now gone.

My coaches ran over to check on me with concerned looks on their faces. Coach Blackman and Coach Powell both said, "Don't worry about it. Your season is not over, and you will be back running fast in no time." When I got home, my roommates all said the same thing. It was encouraging. It made me want to stay in the fight. It was no longer about me. I had to endure this fight for my son and was determined to do just that.

I spent the next few months recovering—receiving treatment for my hamstring twice a day and getting therapy in the pool. It was hard watching my teammates at full strength, while I had a bum tire that needed to be fixed. I continued to see my son with the help of my new girlfriend, Dawn, who I met months before at the local mall. She was kind, sweet, beautiful, and very smart. She was a student at the University of California, Riverside. Because she lived close, we spent lots of time together. She treated my son like he was her own. I could easily see her being my wife because she had all the great qualities of a wife, mother, and best friend.

Coach Blackman was leery of me having an additional distraction with a new girlfriend, but I assured him where my focus lie. After two months of trying to get my body right, I started to get back on the track to do some light workouts. My hamstring seemed to be fully healed, thanks to my coaches. What seemed to be a career-ending injury that had me feeling hopeless, was no longer the case. I was blessed to have a good support system with my mom, track coaches, teammates, and Dawn. Everything was starting to click on all cylinders. I was ready again to compete.

The biggest hurdle most athletes must get over when they get hurt is regaining their mental confidence. Well, mine was back. My first race back, I ran the 400m in 46 seconds. No pain, no issues. My coaches were thrilled and shocked that I ran so fast after pulling my hamstring. Coach Blackman told me from day one, I needed to believe I was a pro athlete, and that's what I did. Although 46 in the 400m was good—it wasn't world-class. I wanted to run at least 43 seconds, and I was fully capable of doing it.

Also, I decided I wanted to distinguish myself from other track runners, so before my first competition back, I pledged to myself I would wear a head band and make that my trademark for the rest of my track and field career. I thought it was a great idea because no matter where I competed around the world, my mom, fans, coaches, and teammates would always be able to identify me.

Even with all the physical and mental conditioning, there was one area of my life I thought was holding me back—my nutrition. Quietly, I still struggled with my eating disorder, but I couldn't tell my coaches because I felt they wouldn't understand. I didn't have a ton of money and neither did my roommates, so we ate lots of rice, mashed potatoes, and eggs. I was tired of being broke, so I decided to get a job at a McDonald's, just down the street from our apartment. My coaches were not on board with me working because they wanted me to focus on school and my track season, but they also understood I had a son to take care of.

My McDonald's job only lasted two weeks. My already demanding schedule just couldn't take it. I knew if I wanted to accomplish my goals that were written everywhere I looked as a constant reminder, I would need to be completely focused on school and track. I became even more focused than ever to run fast. I really wanted to beat Michael Johnson. I kept a picture of Michael in my bedroom as a reminder that I needed to stay the course.

My next competition was in Antelope Valley, and the word was out that I was back in great form and running fast. Antelope Valley had a sprinter who was talented, but in my eyes, he wasn't as talented as me. Coach Blackman told me he didn't want me to wear my spikes for this race. I looked at him like, "Huh?" He didn't believe it was necessary for me to go all out this meet because there was no one to compete with me. I agreed. My mind set was, if I could run fast in my running shoes, imagine what I would do in spikes. I got in the blocks, and the starter gave the commands. When the whistle blew, I took off like a cheetah. Antelope Valley's talented 400m runner took off fast, too, but I let him go and focused on running my own race. We get to the second turn, and I'm feeling relaxed—jaws jiggling like jelly, and then I start to pick it up. The Antelope runner had a slight lead, but I gained on him. When we hit the straightaway, I was behind him a tad, and he ended up crossing the finish line—beating me by a hair. I hate to lose, so that didn't sit well with me at all. The upside was I ran a low 48 seconds in my running shoes. My coaches were all pleased with my performance, and we all knew I was getting ready to dominate in my upcoming meets.

We had many talented ladies on my track team. One, in particular, caught my eye—Chara. Like me, she ran the 400m and 200m. Chara stayed to herself and seemed extremely focused on her schooling and being the best sprinter she could be. Although, I was dating Dawn, I couldn't help noticing Chara. She had all the qualities I liked. She was focused on getting her degree. She was athletic and competitive, and she was very beautiful. Eventually, I pursued Chara. She and I formed a relationship, while Dawn and I broke up.

Everything seemed to be falling into place nicely, and my next meet would be the Riverside Track Classic in my hometown. At the Riverside Track Classic, I dropped 45.7 in the 400m and 21.16 in the 200m, and everyone was shocked. I knew I could run even faster, considering I was getting into race shape. My confidence was at an all-time high. Chara was successfully winning her meets at the same time, which earned us the title, "Super Couple."

As much as I was doing well on the track and in my relationship with Chara, I was still struggling to provide for my son, Malik, who was one year old now. But, I was flat broke, with no car, and I could barely buy him a pack of diapers. Days before the Southern California prelims, I was so upset I couldn't provide for my son, I went out on a late-night run around my neighborhood at 11pm and just cried my eyes out. I prayed to God that He would help change my circumstances, so I could be a provider for Malik. I couldn't wait to compete in the Southern California prelims to show everyone nationwide, I was the new sheriff in town. I won the Southern California prelims with ease in the 400m and 200m. Coach Blackman and I knew there wasn't an athlete in junior college who would be able to beat me. But, I had to stay humble and continue to train as if I weren't the fastest 400m and 200m in junior college. Every time I trained, my thoughts were always on becoming the fastest 400m runner in the world. I made sure I constantly looked over my goals every day, and I trained as hard on the track and in the weight room as if my life depended on it.

We had a big week coming up with the Southern California finals in Bakersfield, and I wanted to have a great weekend of training. I did plenty of speed, endurance, and hill work. I, also, got in some gym time. I did everything in my power to best prepare for the Southern California finals. When we arrived at Bakersfield Community College, and I stepped out of the van, my mind, immediately, went into game mode. I loved watching boxing, and Mike Tyson was my all-time favorite boxer. I loved watching him make his way through the ropes, walking to the center of the boxing ring, sizing up his opponents—looking for any type of weakness to exploit. I had that same type of attitude, but I wasn't in a boxing ring, fighting another man with my fists; my fight was with my feet.

I had a few races to compete in at the finals. My first was the 4X100m relay. When it came time for our team to line up, I could hear the chatter of runners from other teams expressing concern about running against me. I just smiled inside. They were already defeated, and we hadn't run the race yet. As expected, we ended up winning that relay, which qualified us for state.

My legs were now primed and ready for the 400m prelims. Coach Blackman told me I had drawn lane seven, but it didn't matter to me because whatever lane I ran in, I still had to run 400m. I checked into the call room, grabbed my number, and walked onto the track. My headband was tightly fitted around my head, my bodysuit clung to my body like glue, and I felt my blood boiling with rage to unleash all the pain I'd endured onto my competitors. I walked behind my blocks, closed my eyes to visualize my race, and asked God to please bless me to win. The starter yelled, "On your mark, set . . ." My head was up, and I was looking straight down the track, and then the gun went off.

I hold my breath for thirty meters like my coach instructed me, and my cheeks fill up like a balloon. I exhale after the thirty meters and feel this huge surge, allowing my body to run faster. I'd already made up the stagger on the runner in front of me at the 200m mark. I get to 200m and feel this calmness in my body. I'm in the zone, and there's not an inch of pain in my body. I'm racing by myself and don't feel anyone close to me. The second turn, I pick it up as if I were running an open 200m, and that momentum whips on to the last 100m. My arms and legs are pumping with tremendous power, and I cross the finish line with plenty of air in my lungs.

I looked back to see the other runners still battling for position to get second, third, or fourth. Chara was at the finish line waiting and greeted me with a hug and kiss. The crowd got quiet before my time flashed, and then all of a sudden, the announcer blurted out, "New national 400m record 44.52 and the second-fastest time in the world behind Michael Johnson!" Tears of joy began streaming down my face. I had finally accomplished what Coach Blackman and I talked about one year ago. He promised to make me great, and he did.

There wasn't much time for celebration—the 200m was up next, and my goal was to break the 200m national record. My legs were a little fatigued, considering the 400m race was the fastest I had ever run in my life. I checked in for the 200m and was escorted out to the track with all the other 200m runners. I did a couple of starts to make sure my legs were feeling good, and they were. I had to make sure my headband was on, since that had become my new trademark. The starter blew the whistle and gave the commands. I jolted out so quickly that when I looked up, I was already at the 100m mark, getting ready to come in on the homestretch. I could feel the guys next to me huffing and puffing hard to stay with me, but when I got on the homestretch, my 400m strength was too much for them to handle. I crossed the finish line in 20.36, easily winning my prelims. My dreams were starting to become my reality.

When I returned to school on Monday, it seemed the whole college knew about my victory in Bakersfield. My professors were congratulating me, and Coach Blumenthal told me several colleges called to inquire about my university plans. Here I was, back at the top, just like in my senior year of high school. There were several Division 1 universities across the country wanting to offer me a full-ride scholarship. After two years of wandering around the country like a vagabond trying to redeem myself, I had finally arrived at my resting place. Even though I was feeling myself, Coach Blackman was there to keep me humble. I may have *been* the second fastest 400m runner in the world, but he made sure I remained hungry and worked as if I weren't.

In no time, we were traveling back to Bakersfield for the Southern California finals. Since now, I was the best thing since sliced bread, I had to manage my training, along with doing interviews. Because it seemed as if I were dropped from the sky, everyone wanted to know where I came from. Little did they know, I was always there. I just had a GPS error which took me in the wrong direction. If everything had gone according to plan, instead of competing at the Southern California finals, I would now be a sophomore at the University of Oregon, starting my second season as a starter. Life is very unpredictable. When you think you have it all planned out, God stops you in your tracks and says, "I have another plan for you which is ten times better than the one you have."

The day before my track meet, I was nervous. I thought much about my son and what I could do to make the world championship team and win a gold in the 400m. Competing in junior college was a means to an end, so I could move one step closer to competing against the world's best. We left for the Southern California finals early in the morning, and Chara was right there with me in the van for our long journey. Coach Blackman made sure I stayed calm and didn't overthink my race. I had the tendency to overthink things, which affected my practice—and sometimes my race.

We arrived back in Bakersfield with enough time to rest and get ready for the 4X100m relay. When the time came for us to be escorted onto the track, I looked up at the stands. I was amazed at the number of people who were there to see the Southern California finals. As I walked to my spot on the track, I could hear people chanting 43, 43, 43. I couldn't believe so many people came to see me run. It was like I was a rock star. I was excited about running the relay, but I couldn't wait to run the 400m. We came in second in the relay, which qualified us for state.

As my mind shifted gears to my 400m, I felt the whole world was watching me and waiting to see if I was going to run 43 seconds in the 400m. I knew 43 wasn't going to happen because Coach Blackman didn't want a 43 that day. He made it clear, to run a fast 280m and then coast all the way to the finish line. I was one of the last 400m runners to walk up and check in at the call room. When I did walk up, I could see the fear in every runner I was competing against. They were already defeated from hearing about me and seeing the time I ran last week, so this race wasn't about me competing against them; it was me competing against myself and the clock. I won both the 400m and the 200m, which made me the heavy favorite to win them both at state.

One week down, and one more to go to close out my Cinderella track season. I could see the light at the end of the tunnel, and it felt as if I were being reborn. I was happy with where my life was going. It felt great to be wanted again by universities. Coach Blumenthal would tell me almost every day that college coaches from major Division 1 universities were calling to find out if I wanted to play football, run track, or do both in college. I had many recruiters come to my apartment, attempting to recruit me for their school. Because I had already been through the recruiting process in high school, I knew their pitch. I had better judgement the second time around in deciding whether I wanted to go back to college or go professional in track and field. I knew whatever decision I made; it would have to benefit my son.

I was at peace the week of the junior college track and field state meet. I had already proven I could run world-class times, so I was confident going into the meet. My training was all about sharpening up, relaxing, and having fun. I was in the best shape of my life. Coach Blackman told me to stay out of the weight room, but I couldn't. I loved to bench press, and I would lift as much as 275 pounds just to make sure I had lots of power in my upper body.

To my surprise, Chara's parents decided to make the drive the Fresno, CA to see me compete. I knew Chara would be there but having her parents there, too, was a win-win for me.

When we arrived in Fresno, per my normal routine, I went for a jog and stretched, so I could loosen up after a long drive. I did some interviews after dinner, which reinforced the public's expectation—that I would run 43 in the 400m. The world was watching, and I wondered if Michael Johnson was watching, too. At the time, Michael Johnson was the fastest 400m and 200m runner on planet earth. He wore the golden track spikes in the 1996 Olympics, broke the world record in the 200m, and broke the Olympic record in the 400m. If destiny would bring us together, Michael and I would compete against each other at the 1997 World Outdoor Championships in Athens, Greece.

The day of the race, the stadium was jam-packed with people, including the media and news reporters. I loved big crowds, and I channeled their energy for my race. My first race was the 4X100. Once again, as we walked into the call room, I could sense the fear in our competitors. We didn't end up winning the 4X100, but we did our best. Next up was my race, the 400m. As I walked back to the warm-up area, I shouted to the crowd, "43, here it comes!" I went to stretch my legs and relax for a while to get completely focused on running my race.

After resting for a while, it was time to get ready for the 400m. My heart was racing, and my stomach was turning, but I was ready to deliver a mighty blow to my competitors and let the world know that a junior college boy could be the best and fastest 400m runner in the world. I did a light warmup and then walked over to the call room to get my lane and number. I felt my competitors didn't want to race me at all, but I couldn't allow cockiness to deter my focus of simply competing against myself and to run the way I'd been running all year. I walked the track with all my competitors, and I could hear people chanting, "43, 43, 43!" Amid the cheers, I could hear Chara rooting for me.

I walked over to my lane, took off my sweats, made sure my headband was on right, and my blocks were set the right way. When the starter blew the first whistle for everyone to line up behind their blocks, I closed my eyes and asked God to allow me to win my race and finish without injury. I saw myself running and winning the race before it happened, and then when I opened my eyes, the starter said, "Runners, on your marks." My heart beat like a drum, and my stomach churned like the ocean. I looked straight ahead, with one knee touching the track and one foot in the blocks. I hear the next command, "Set." I'm up; my body slightly leaning forward while I'm holding my breath, and then the gun goes off. I'm out so fast, and one by one, I'm passing my competitors as if they're standing still. The noise from the crowd is growing. I get to 200m, and I know I'm on pace to run 43. My competitors start to fade back more and more at 250m, and then I make my final kick. When I see the finish line in my sight, my body starts to get tight, but inside I'm telling myself, "No Ty; push through!". That's when I hit the finish line. When I looked at the timer, it read, 44.91. I was extremely disappointed because I knew I could've run faster than that. But, I didn't have time to sit and sulk. I had to prepare for my 200m.

The crowd, though, went crazy when they saw my time, but I knew my Cinderella season was almost complete. After my race, I ran over to Chara and gave her a big hug. She told me she was proud of me, and her parents also congratulated me. What put a smile on my face was seeing my coaches and teammates on cloud nine that I was bringing a state title back to San Bernardino Valley College.

There was talk that some athletes from Northern California were going to upset me in the 200m. I knew I had a big bullseye on my chest, but I was always up for the challenge. The humidity was super high in Fresno, and I started to cramp up while I was resting in the warm-up area. I told Coach Powell my legs were cramping, and if it didn't go away, it was going to be difficult to run the 200m. Coach Powell went to get me some Gatorade, and I drank that while stretching out my legs. I knew I was going to have to get out really fast, and I couldn't afford to have any type of cramping. I only had a short time to rest.

Sure enough, after taking a quick break, I had to get up and do some stretching and jogging. My calves felt like rocks but backing out from competing was not in my DNA. I heard a call over the microphone for all 200m runners to report to the call room. I walked over to get my number, but I didn't want to let anyone know I was in pain. That would be like being a wounded animal waiting for predators to devour you. I walked over to my lane, set the blocks, and then took off my sweat suit to do one start off the blocks to see how I felt. My legs still felt tight after doing one start, but I had to block out the pain and pretend nothing was wrong with me. Unlike the 400m, there were some good 200m runners who were pure sprinters. They would try with all their might to keep me from beating them. The starter blew the whistle for us to get ready. I stood behind my blocks with my eyes closed and prayed to God, He would take away my pain and allow me to be victorious in my last junior college race.

The starter's commands set my heart racing, and then the gun went off. I'm not out as fast as I wanted, but then my legs turned over like pistons. My competitors were grunting and trying with all their might to pull away from me, but they couldn't. When we got to the last 100m, my 400m strength kicked in, and one by one, the other runners faded. I was all alone when I crossed the finish line—victorious in my last junior college race.

I, immediately, looked over to the timer, and it said 20.30, a new junior college state record. Coach Powell was in shock because he knew there had been a chance I would have to pull out of the race because of cramping. But, I decided to finish what I started. I was tired and happy at the same time. All the hard work I put in for months with my coaches had finally paid off. Now, I was known not only in California but all over the world.

Chara was in tears. She was so happy for me, and we hugged for what seemed like forever. My son was too young to understand the magnitude of what I just did, but his life was going to change for the better. My dream was to become a state champion, and it came true. I never gave up on pursuing my dream even when others couldn't catch the vision. I was the happiest I had been in a long time. But, it was also a bittersweet time because I was closing the chapter on my junior college track season.

Chapter 10

My Destiny

My junior college track and field season was over, and I had to get my mind prepared for the US Outdoor National Championships in Indianapolis. I would be racing the top 400m runners in the world to try and secure a spot for the World Championships in Athens, Greece. I was ready to compete against anybody because Coach Blackman ingrained in me early that I had nothing to fear.

Roger Lipkis, the team manager of my track and field club, West Valley Eagles, got in touch with me and asked if I had thought about becoming a professional in track and field. I said if I could make the World Outdoor Championship team and get a million-dollar contract, I would consider it. Coach Blackman and I discussed my going pro many times but getting my degree was especially important. If I got my degree and got hurt running, I would still be able to get a good job—coaching in college or working for some major organization. I shared with Coach Blackman that Roger wanted to manage me, and he was fine with it, as long as I didn't accept any money. If I would've accepted money, that would have essentially disqualified me from getting a full scholarship to a Division 1 university.

I couldn't wait to get on the track to battle the world's best at the Outdoor Nationals, like Butch Reynolds, Antonio Pettigrew, and Michael Johnson. They were all runners I'd heard about in the news. Roger connected me with Mark Crear, and when we met for the first time, it was as if I had known him all my life. I looked up to him because he was coming off a great year—winning silver at the summer Olympics in Atlanta. He knew what it would take to become great. He, instantly, took me under his wing as his little brother, and I remember him asking me if I had a suit. I told him I could never afford a suit, so he gave me one of his. I lit up like a kid in a candy store—not only would I be training with an Olympic silver medalist, I would also look the part by being professionally dressed when I left for the Outdoor Nationals. Mark and I trained together at College of the Canyons in Santa Clarita, and it was a quiet place to concentrate and critique my race. After a couple weeks of training, Roger, Mark, and I traveled to Indianapolis for the Outdoor Nationals.

I knew making the world championship team would change my life forever. If I didn't make it this year, I would have to wait another full year to win a US National Championship. At this point, I had done all I could do physically and mentally to be ready.

It was amazing to see so many Olympians and world champions walking around the venue, wearing their sponsored gear, and signing autographs. It felt good knowing I'd be sharing a platform with some of the best athletes in the world.

The morning of my race, I went to the practice track to warm up and do block starts. Many of my competitors were also warming up on the track, and I couldn't help watching them try and exploit any weakness I might have. A lot of eyes were on me because I came out of nowhere, according to the track statisticians. When the time was nearing to get ready to go to the track to prepare for my first heat of the 400m, I made sure I had my CD player with "My Love is Your Love," by Whitney Houston locked in. "My Love is Your Love" was my favorite song to listen to before a competition because I needed something to calm me down, since I was extremely hyper. I had never met Whitney Houston, but I loved her soothing voice, which always put me at ease. When I checked in for my race, I was given lane seven because I had the second fastest time in the world. It didn't matter what lane we were placed in, we all had 400 meters to run.

When the starter blew the whistle for all runners to get ready, I took off my tights, put on my trademark headband, and got in the blocks to wait for the commands. The starter gave all the commands, the gun went off, and I was on my way. Coach Blackman told me to blast my 300m, make sure I maintained the lead, and then coast home. So, I got a fast start, and before I knew it, I was jogging my last hundred, qualifying for the second round. I walked off the track, and reporters were asking me how I felt. I told them I felt good and looked forward to the next round. I dominated in the semi-finals, and the world was seeing I wasn't a fluke but the real deal. The finals were going to be a showdown between some of the greatest 400m runners in the world, and I was ready.

When I spoke with Coach Blackman about the final, he told me it was my race to win and that none of the 400m runners had enough speed, strength, and mental toughness to beat me. I believed him. The whole world would be watching the 400m final, and I was ready to take my crown, as I had planned to do for many months. I went through my usual routine, which included shaving my head and legs, laying out my uniform, and saying a prayer to God. I wanted so badly for God to hear my prayer, so I could win the US Outdoor Nationals, which would change my life forever.

There are many good athletes in the world, but there are not many athletes who reach the point of greatness. My journey to this point was rough, but the opportunity which lay before me would put me on the path toward greatness. God knew the desires of my heart, and on the day of the final, He delivered. Despite the many other great athletes present that day, I finished second and made the World Outdoor Championship team!

I was on cloud nine. Millions of people all over the world witnessed a junior college athlete, who'd endured many trials and tribulations, become runner-up at the US Outdoor National Championships in the 400m. I did many interviews with news reporters, sharing my long journey to get to the US Championships. Roger was ecstatic that I was runner-up at the US Nationals in my very first attempt. Because of my second-place finish, Nike offered me a two-year deal with good money, although the exact figure wasn't discussed yet. Reebok was also on the table. And, if I placed in the top three at the World Championships, I could secure even more money. I took my time deciding who to sign with and to decide whether I should wait to go pro until after the World Championships in Athens, Greece. I was so grateful God blessed me to accomplish something most people thought was impossible. I was the best 400m runner in the US!

After taking in my victory, now it was time to prepare for the European track and field circuit and get ready to battle the rest of the top 400m runners in the world. My first competition was in Paris, France, against Michael Johnson. I had been waiting for this moment for so long, but I wanted to race Michael in the US not in Europe—a place I had no familiarity with. I had never been overseas, and I was terrified to travel to another country. But, if that was what I had to do to be the best in the world, then so be it.

After a long and tiresome flight, I finally arrived in Paris. The weather was horrible! When I left Los Angeles, it was almost 90 degrees—in Paris, the high was in the 40's, and it was raining. I couldn't believe how gloomy it was, but I was also taken by the beautiful architecture all around me. The first chance I got, I purchased a prepaid phone card, so I could call back home. I called Chara and my mom back in the states and was nearly in tears, telling them how I disliked Paris. I told them I didn't like the food, and the people seemed rude to me because I didn't speak French. My mom and Chara told me to stick it out, and that's what I planned to do. After the calls, I felt much better, and the homesickness I was feeling went away.

When I checked into my hotel, I immediately hurried to my room to use the bathroom, but there was no tissue. Instead, they had two toilets. I had never seen anything like that in my life! I figured out after some investigation, one toilet was for handling your business, and the other one was to wash your behind. I was simply amazed at how French people needed two toilets – one to do their business and one to wash their behind!

Next, on my itinerary was to pick up my packet, so I could get my meal tickets, race schedule, bib number, practice times at the track, and schedule for the technical meeting. Everything sounded good except for the technical meeting. I had no idea what that was, so I asked around. The technical meeting is a meeting with agents, discussing lane assignments for their athletes. Since Roger wasn't with me, I attended the technical meeting against the wishes of other agents and coaches. My sentiment was I had to speak up for myself or nobody else would. I had been doing that all my life. I was already branded the new kid on the block who had a chip on his shoulder—and they were right. I came from a tough upbringing, and I had to fight for everything I had, so I wasn't about to let people I didn't know dictate my future.

I knew Michael was the king of the 400m, and it was a given he would have whatever lane he wanted. I was the second best 400m runner in the world, so I wanted to make sure I would have the next best lane on the track. When the lane assignments were posted later that evening, I was in a good lane, and that's the way I wanted it to be. I might be the new kid on the block, but I wasn't going to let anyone run all over me.

After all the anticipation and months of waiting, the day finally arrived for me to battle the man the world was talking about. Michael was king of the 400m, and what he did the following year at the 1996 Olympics in the 400m and 200m was extraordinary. I didn't get caught up in the hype and was fully aware that when Michael stepped on the track, he would be ready to show the world why he's the 400m king. I would be racing later in the evening, so I had to balance my time resting, eating, and walking a little bit to keep loose. The sand in the hourglass was getting to its last drop, and that meant it was time for me to show the world that I was no fluke.

We arrived at the stadium, and it was amazing! US Nationals was a big deal and seeing the French crowd and people from all over the world was surreal. As soon as I stepped off the charter bus, there were many fans asking for autographs, and vendors everywhere selling memorabilia. The crowd seemed so big, I thought I was at the World Championships. People seemed like they couldn't care less that it was cold, gloomy, and raining. I loved the energy that circulated around the stadium.

When Michael walked in, it seemed the other 400m runners were very timid. I could see in their eyes, that yet again, they were already defeated before the race even began. I was out for blood and didn't care what he did at the 1996 Olympics or years before. It was amazing to hear the roar of the fans, and sport reporters everywhere, to see some of the best athletes in the world compete. My goal was to block out all the noise and imagine the stadium empty, with my coach standing in the middle of the field like I was doing a time trial.

I walked up to my lane and set my starting blocks, while the cold and rain pierced my body all over. I took my sweats off. My spikes were soaking up water like a sponge, and my toes seemed to be going numb. I tried hard to block out my discomfort, so I could do two practice starts. Eventually, the starter blew the whistle for the runners to get behind their blocks. The announcer, with his French accent, announced each athlete's first and last name, country, and their personal best time in the 400m. When the starter blew the whistle and said, "Runners, on your mark," at that point, my toes were fully numb.

I took off like lightning and felt good. I told myself to maintain my composure and just run my race. I got to the second 200m and was within striking distance to make my move. I could feel Michael and another runner picking up the pace, so at 150m to go, I made my move. As I got to the final 100m, Michael started to fade. I got to the finish line and finished second behind Davis Kamoga. Michael Johnson's fifty-eight meet winning streak had just come to an end. I was the youngest 400m runner to break his winning streak. I felt validated that I could compete with the best 400m runners in any place around the world. I made my mark on international soil, and my professional career in track and field was no longer a "what if." Now, it was a reality.

Coach Blackman told me during fall training, I could beat Michael, and that's what I did. He also ingrained in me that whether it was a good meet or a bad one, I needed to have a short-term memory. There was no sense dwelling on what happened in the race (win or lose) because it was over. That was my mentality because now I had to prepare for my next race, which was in Lille, France, where I would run the 200m. The 200m was a great race for me because it helped me work on my speed for the 400m.

I started getting to know other athletes in Paris and that helped me feel more comfortable being in Europe. When I arrived in Lille, like Paris, it was gloomy and cold. My asthma was acting up and breathing that cold air didn't help my lungs at all. I always had to keep my rescue inhaler on me because I could have an asthma attack anytime, anywhere. Asthma was my kryptonite, but I never let my sickness stop me from getting what I wanted.

One night, I couldn't sleep, and I ran into Alvin Harrison, a silver-medalist from the 1996 Olympics in Atlanta, Georgia. He and his identical twin, Calvin, both ran the 400m. Their life story was broadcast all over the world. They endured many hardships, and I felt we had much in common. I introduced myself, and he knew who I was. We ended up talking for hours, well into the night about life. We had so much in common. We trained together, ate together, and seemed to be like two peas in a pod.

The day of my race I was ready, and I felt none of my competitors could beat me—not even the up-and-coming, Maurice Green, who ran the 100m and was projected to be the next great US sprinter. Most of the time, people didn't believe a 400m runner could be a force in the 200m. Usually, the 100m and 200m runners dominated those events. Michael Johnson changed that perception after the 1996 Olympics, and I was going to do the same.

As expected, it was raining and cold, but it didn't matter to me because I was extremely focused on blocking out anything and everything that would hinder my performance. When the starter blew the whistle for all runners to have their sweats and tights off, I was behind my blocks with my eyes closed, visualizing my race before it happened. In my mind, I had already won. I just needed to perform my duty and collect my reward.

I came out like lightning, and Maurice and I both hit the final straightaway faster than the blink of an eye. I crossed the finish line with my arms spread wide, smiling for all the cameras. I congratulated everyone, but Maurice seemed to be upset about losing to a 400m runner.

My final meet in Europe was in Lausanne, Switzerland, where the weather would be the same as in Lille. The 400m lineup was going to be loaded, with the 400m world record holder, Butch Reynolds, in the race. I beat Butch Reynolds at the US Outdoor Nationals, and I was sure he wanted a rematch. He got what he wanted. Despite the pouring rain, he ran 43, and I ran 44, placing second. I'll never forget, after we both crossed the finish line, Butch turned to me and said, "Welcome to the big league, rookie." I was like, "Whoa!" A good reminder that I wasn't in college anymore and would have to man up.

Butch was good to me. He schooled me plenty about how the European circuit worked, who to trust, and who to stay away from. I grew up running the street and knew it very well but being on the track circuit was different. I needed to learn the business side of track and field, and Butch gave me the insight. My time in Europe came to an end, and it was a reality check for me. I had never been out of the US prior to this trip. I never even imagined I would be walking around Paris, France, competing against athletes from all over the world. It was an amazing experience, and I wanted more experiences like it.

I had a tough decision to make—whether to take the prize money I made in the European track and field meets or deny the money and accept a scholarship to a major university. I thought about my current situation. I was struggling to buy diapers, clothes, and formula for my son. I had no car and no home of my own, so I decided to take the money and become a professional track and field athlete.

I stayed with Roger and Des while I prepared for the World Outdoor Championships in Athens, Greece. I knew if I wanted to become a world champion, I would have to be mentally stronger than any 400m runner in the world. The downside of preparing for the World Championships was the limited time I had with Malik and Chara. In order to be the world's best 400m runner, I couldn't let any distractions get in my way.

It was a long flight to Greece, but I had a business-class ticket, which was great. It was my first time sitting in the front of the plane, because I could never afford it. I was happy to have extra leg room.

I slept through most of the flight, and before I knew it, the captain, said "Flight attendants, prepare for arrival." I was so excited to be in Greece! I couldn't believe I was going to compete in the country where the Olympics originated. The moment I walked off the plane, it was a frenzy with world championship banners and pictures of all the athletes.

Jerome Young was an up-and-coming 400m runner like me, and we became instant friends. He, too, was a junior college product and was running really fast. We both were planning to spoil Michael Johnson's plans to repeat as world champ. I was advised it was mandatory we attend the opening ceremonies. However, Coach Blackman advised against it because I had to run early in the morning, and he didn't want me to be on my feet for a long period of time the day before. I took his advice. Instead of attending the opening ceremonies, I stayed in my room, watched movies on my laptop, and listened to music on my CD player.

The next morning, I had to get my mind right to run two rounds in one day. As usual, I laid out all my equipment and shaved my legs, armpits, near my groin, and my head. I didn't want any hair on my body except for my mustache and eyebrows. Having a smooth shaved body made me feel as if I could run extremely fast, and that was a feeling I craved. I was still struggling with bulimia. Whenever I felt too full after eating a meal, I would throw it up, so I could perform well on the track.

I didn't want to run the 400m an all-out performance because I had another run later in the evening. I was the second fastest 400m runner in the world, so I knew I would get a good lane for the first round. I ran the first round just as we scripted it, and I won with so much ease. I felt like I was *walking* the last hundred meters, and I could see my competitors behind me on the big screen, struggling. I finished my race and was interviewed about how I felt. I told the reporters I felt great and was looking forward to running the quarterfinals. Jerome and Antonio Pettigrew advanced too, so all our 400m runners were still in the hunt for the gold.

It was time for the quarterfinals, and it seemed as though many critics, fans, coaches, and agents didn't think I would survive the demanding four rounds, but I was about to prove them wrong. I ran my quarterfinal race with much ease to advance to the semifinals. The semifinals would be much tougher than the previous rounds, and I needed to stay focused, so I could be in a great position to win the world championship. I was poised and ready when I stepped on the track for my semifinals. Before the start of my race, I closed my eyes, visualized myself hitting my marks at each hundred meters, and said a quick prayer, asking God to let me get through my race healthy, and win my heat. I ran a fantastic semi-final race, easing up just before the finish line—letting the packed crowd know there was a new sheriff in town. Reporters swarmed me after my semi-final race and asked me if I thought Michael Johnson was capable of reigning as the 400m king. I said I didn't think he could continue his dominance.

The finals were going to be epic—with three Americans and three Brits, with Michael Johnson favored to win. I was aiming to change that outcome. When I walked into the stadium for the 400m final, the crowd was roaring like a tornado. My stomach churned from nervousness. The moment had finally arrived to show the world I was the best 400m runner in the world.

I stood behind my blocks, rolling my neck, shrugging my shoulders, and quietly asking God to let me win the race and become the 400m world champion. I got into the blocks, and before I knew it, the gun went off, and I was lunging out of the blocks like a greyhound dog coming out the gate. My body felt good as I entered my second 200, and I knew I should have kicked at 180 meters like Coach Blackman wanted me to. Instead, I waited until about 150 meters. My last hundred was always strong, but it was too late. Michael crossed the finish line first, repeating as world champion, while I placed third for a bronze medal.

My first thought was, "Why didn't you kick at 180 meters because you would have won gold?" It was a lesson learned for my future races, and I was happy to be on the podium at all—considering I was still in junior college.

Many reporters and critics were shocked I medaled at the World Championships my first year. Two years prior, I had signed a full-ride scholarship to the University of Oregon to play football. When that didn't pan out, I traveled the country like a vagabond, trying to salvage my athletic career. But, enrolling at San Bernardino Valley College in the winter of 1996 and working with Coach Blackman, changed my life. When you believe in yourself, set your goals, visualize where you want to be, and train to be what you want to be, you will become unstoppable. People will witness your greatness with shock and awe.

When I came home, I had some money in my pocket after winning so many meets. I bought a car, and Chara and I went apartment hunting. We found a place in Chino Hills and settled there. I was extremely happy because my son and I would have a place of our own, and Chara could come over as much as she wanted to visit me. I was finally able to start supporting Malik financially on a consistent basis, which brought everything full circle.

Chara and I became closer than we'd ever been, and even though we were fairly young, I asked her if she would marry me, and she said, "Yes." I knew we would get backlash from her parents and my family because we were young, but I didn't care about anybody's opinions. I felt Chara's mom, especially, might be an issue because she didn't consider my profession as a track and field runner a real career, which was disappointing. But, I didn't waver about wanting to marry Chara.

One day, Chara and I were invited to a formal event in which I had to wear a tie, but I had no idea had to tie one! On our way to the event, as we drove through the neighborhood, I saw a white man outside watering his lawn. I told Chara I was going to ask him to teach me how to tie a tie. She looked at me as if I were crazy, asking a random man to show me how to tie a tie. I told her to pull over. I approached the man and said, "Sir, I'm going to an event, and I never had a father in my life to teach me how to tie a tie, so could you help me?" He turned off his water hose, dropped it on the grass, and with a big smile on his face, replied, "Sure, I can help you." He took my tie, put it around his neck, and gave me step by step instructions to make a good tie. After he was done making the tie, he took it off his neck, wrapped it around my neck, and adjusted it nicely to fit my dress shirt. Chara was in awe. I shook the man's hand and thanked him for helping me and treating me as if I were his own son who was preparing to go to the prom. That moment in time taught me a lot about life. Even though, I didn't have a father in my life, there were plenty of men willing to step in and treat me like their very own child.

Chapter 11

The San Diego Chargers

I dreamed of becoming a professional football player ever since my days in the Riverside Junior Tackle Football League. Whenever I played pick-up football with the kids in my neighborhood, at school, at practice, or in my football games, I imagined myself being Eric Dickerson or Walter Payton. My friends and teammates would ask me, "Who are you today, Tyree?" I would say, "I'm Eric Dickerson." The next time I would say, "I'm Walter Payton." Every Sunday, I watched NFL football and was glued to the television to see how well Eric and Walter would do, running the football. I tried mimicking Walter's running style whenever I ran the ball.

Walter Payton played for the Chicago Bears, who won a Super Bowl in the '80s. He was about 5'10," with 204 pounds of chiseled muscle. He looked like a superhero that was sent from above. When Walter ran with the football, he would pause, and then he would hit another gear, slipping through the cracks of defenders, running them over, and scoring touchdowns. Walter was known as, "Sweetness" because as one reporter said, "He runs so sweet that it gives me cavities just watching him." I wanted to be him in every way.

Eric Dickerson played for the Los Angeles Rams in the early '80s, and I admired how graceful and fluid he was when he ran the football. He had a tall slender build that seemed like he was made of steel. He had a long Jheri-curl and wore goggles, with a neck brace around his shoulder pads. I loved how he navigated his way around the football field, ducking and dodging defenders, while he ate up yards, scoring touchdowns. I wanted to be just like two of my favorite running backs in the NFL, so every time I got the opportunity to run the football, I was running over defenders, doing Sweetness' pause and burst move, and running down the sideline, scoring touchdowns.

In 1998, I was coming off a stellar athletic performance in track and field, winning two silver medals at the Goodwill Games, and at the time, breaking the world record in the 4X400m relay. After breaking the world record in the relay, a reporter from *USA Today* asked me, "Ty, what's next for your track and field career?" I said, "I'm going to play football in the NFL." The reporter looked amazed at my reply because I just won two silver medals and broke a world record in track. Even though I had accomplished a great deal in my athletic career, my heart was in playing pro football not in track and field.

In 1999, I hired Dr. Harold Daniels aka Doc, who was a well-known agent for the National Football League (NFL). Doc managed many NFL players that were drafted or picked up as free agents. During the 1999 season, I still had a contract with Reebok, and my plan was to run more 200-meter races to build up my stamina for my NFL workouts. I ran 20.09, which was a personal best, in May of 1999 at the Jackie Joyner meet in East Saint Louis, and I felt great! I could bench press 225 pounds more than ten times, and I could easily dunk a basketball, standing still underneath the rim. At my first meeting with Doc, he asked me if I was in football shape, and I told him I was a little rusty but to give me some time, and I would be ready to do any defensive back or receiver drill that any NFL coaches threw at me.

I figured my track and field workouts would take care of my speed and conditioning. The only other thing I would need to do was practice my route-running and defensive back drills. Doc had an assistant, JJ Flournoy, who was in the Riverside area where I resided, and he came out to help me with agility, route-running, and defensive back drills. After about a month of training, working on defensive back and receiver drills, I was ready for NFL workouts. Doc told me to attend an open NFL workout at Mount San Antonio College where some NFL scouts would be.

I had a morning workout, and I was extremely nervous because this one performance was my opportunity, and my chances of playing in the NFL could be over in the blink of an eye. I did the normal track and field warmup. The NFL scouts from the Baltimore Ravens, New York Giants, Arizona Cardinals, Green Bay Packers, and the Oakland Raiders were all lined up on the track to time the forty-yard dash. I blazed a 4.34 in the cold, and I decided not to run anymore because I didn't want to risk pulling a muscle. Next, I did a couple of defensive back and receiver drills on the grass, and just like that, it was over. You spend more time putting in training hours than you do for your workout in front of scouts!

I called Doc and told him about my workout, and he was pleased. He said this workout should open more doors for me to get additional workouts with NFL scouts and lead me to, eventually, signing with an NFL team. When I got home, I told my wife, Chara, about my workout. I kept telling her how nervous I was, but she said, "You're always nervous before a workout." She was right! A week went by, and I got a call from Doc, telling me the San Diego Chargers and the Oakland Raiders wanted to work me out.

I was excited about both workouts because both teams were from California, and I would be close to my three-year-old son Malik. Malik's mother and I had shared custody. I drove down to San Diego in my SUV on the I-15 freeway, listening to music and visualizing what the San Diego Chargers' coaches were going to ask me to do.

When I arrived at the Chargers' facility, I was in awe, looking up at the wall at so many great players who came before me that had taken the same path to become a San Diego Charger. I met with the coaches, and they directed me to the gym to go change into Chargers' gear. My first workout was in the weight room, and the strength and conditioning coach, John Hastings, took me through some challenging workouts that really tested my weaknesses. Considering my weight room workouts were geared towards track and field, I did a rather good job with impressing the strength and conditioning coach. After the weight room, I took a break, and then shortly after, the director of personnel, Greg Gaines, told me I needed to go onto the football field to do receiver and defensive back drills.

I walked to the back of the facility where the turf football field was located, and I put on my cleats. The first route I ran was overthrown by the quarterback, so I dove to try and get a one-handed catch, but I came up short. I jumped up and ran, and the QB said, "My fault." Everyone was looking down at my arm, so I looked down, too and realized that landing on the turf had scraped a large piece of skin off my arm. The coaches told me to get bandaged and cleaned up, so I did and came right back to finish my workout.

After I was done with everything, Greg told me to go see Bobby Beathard, the general manager for the San Diego Chargers, in his office. I didn't know what Bobby was going to say. I thought my workout was great, but I didn't know if the coaches felt the same way. Bobby said he liked my workout, and if I didn't get picked up in the supplemental draft on July 8, 1999, the Chargers would sign me to a contract. My agent explained to me the supplemental draft was for underclassmen who become ineligible for the college football season after the deadline to enter the NFL's regular draft.

The supplemental draft was July 8th, and I had high hopes I would get picked up by one of the thirty-two teams. Doc said he would keep me informed, but none of the thirty-two teams picked me that day. So, on July 12th, I signed with the San Diego Chargers. That was one of the happiest days of my life. Ever since I was a little boy, my dream was to become a professional football player, and now that dream became a reality. I wore a suit and a red tie that had all the NFL teams on it, and my wife stood right next to me in Bobby's office, as I inked my name on my first NFL contract. To sweeten the deal, Doc negotiated for an $18,000 signing bonus because of my status as a world champion and a world record holder in track and field.

We started training camp in July of 1999 at the University of California, San Diego. I went into the training room at UCSD and got fitted for a helmet and shoulder pads and received my football pants and pads. As the team trainer was fitting me for my helmet, I was smiling inside because my dream had come true. I wanted the number 25 for practice and for my game jerseys because my mother's birthday was August 25th. I didn't get the number I wanted.

Instead, I got jersey number 32. Before training camp, Bobby Beathard promised my agent, Doc, I would play defensive back or free safety, but first, they wanted to try me out at wide receiver. I wasn't happy about that, considering I was bred to play defensive back, but my attitude was to make the best of my situation.

During training camp, we were assigned roommates, and it was mandatory we didn't leave our room past curfew. My roommates were Jay and Bryan. I called Bryan, B-Still. My boy, Jay was a veteran who played previously for the New York Jets. Dick, the head of security, went to every dorm at UCSD and asked every player their name and to show some skin—meaning he needed to see part of your body to make sure you were in bed. I was a newlywed who had married less than a year prior, and the first day in the dorms, I was missing my wife. I had a plan to tell Dick I would stay there until he did his rounds, but after that, I planned to jump in my truck and drive over an hour to see my wife and spend the night with her. My roommates told me I better make sure Dick didn't come back to the room because I would get fined for violating team rules. I never got caught, but I always felt paranoid sneaking out, knowing that if Dick did a room check, I was in deep trouble!

The first day of training camp was a WOW moment. I was all dressed up in my Chargers' gear, walking through a little tunnel heading to the football field on the UCSD campus. I felt on top of the world, knowing this was my first NFL training camp, and that coaches, photographers, and news writers would be following my every move. When you're in camp, it's every man for himself, and there weren't too many players who would help a rookie. Quite frankly, if you were a rookie, you had to hold the veterans' helmets while walking to practice every day. One of the veterans asked me to hold his helmet, but I had a chip on my shoulder, and I wasn't going to hold anyone's helmet. In my eyes, I was a world champion and world record holder in track and field, with many TV appearances all over the world. I wasn't going to hold anyone's helmet!

I met Roderick, who had already been with the Minnesota Vikings' and Dallas Cowboys' camps. He and Jeff, who played for the New York Giants, were the elders of the group. It felt good to be around them, and I knew I would get some good feedback during practice, and when we watched our film. We had ninety players who were all battling for a spot on the fifty-three-man roster. Sirr Parker, who went to high school in Los Angeles and attended Texas A & M University, was a force to be reckoned with. I watched him play college ball, and he was a dynamic running back that could destroy a defense. What also stood out to me about Sirr was his name. There was a rumor in camp that Sirr had his own Blockbuster movie. I couldn't believe it, until one day, I went to Blockbuster with my wife and asked the clerk, "Do you have a movie called, *They Call Me Sirr*?" Sure enough, it was true. I rented his movie and found out he had a challenging upbringing, like myself. His mother named him Sirr because no matter where he traveled around the world, people would always have to call him Sirr, which, immediately, commanded respect. Sirr channeled all the bad energy into doing great academically and athletically to succeed in life. I had lots of respect for Sirr. Like me, he had a child he was taking care of while he was in camp. There was a great deal of pressure to be perfect in camp. You, literally, had no room for error, or you would be sent packing in the blink of an eye.

When I signed with the Chargers, I thought, "Man, I'm going to be playing with Mr. San Diego, Junior Seau." Junior was a star linebacker on our team, and he was liked by so many San Diegans because of his love for the city, his humility, and his foundation which helped many disadvantaged kids in San Diego. The first time I met Junior was in the training room; he was on the training table getting rubbed out. His favorite words were, "Hey buddy." I replied, "Hello Junior!" He then said to me, "You're Tyree Washington. You played at Riverside Community College, and you're one of the fastest men in the world." I was like, Whoa! I asked him, "How did you know that?" He replied, "It's my job to know that! You're now part of this team, and you're also part of my family!" Nothing against my former teammates, but no one made me feel at home more than Junior did!

On one occasion during training camp when I was playing slot receiver, Jim Harbaugh was in at quarterback because we were going live against the first-string defense. As I was in my wide receiver stance, Jim yelled out the cadence, getting everyone in position. I looked over at Junior and Eric, and they are posted up like two Greek statues. Junior was high-strung all the time, running up to the defense line trying to anticipate the count, and then running back. Jim gave the "Hut," and the ball snapped. I took off like lightning and ran a slant route, while Jim did his two-step drop and fired the ball at me as if he were playing darts, trying to hit a bull's eye. I caught the football right as I made my cut, and as soon as I turned my head to go up field, Junior was right there waiting to deliver death to me. I braced for the hit. Junior just shrugged his shoulders and let me run upfield for a touchdown. The cornerbacks and free safety tried to pursue me, but that was like trying to catch a cheetah while you're riding on a skateboard.

I asked Junior after practice why he didn't hit me, and he said, "You're the fastest man in the NFL. If I hurt you, how is that going to help our team?" I was amazed again! Junior was a natural-born leader who took care of his family. I may not have played years in the NFL or made a roster at this stage, but he treated me as if I'd played years in the NFL and was a veteran like him. I love Junior for the respect he gave me and for showing me that family is everything, and it doesn't matter how many years you played in the NFL, how you look, or where you come from. At the end of the day, family is being there for each other during the good times and bad.

We had some challenging times during training camp. My wide receiver coach, Mike Sanford was a new NFL coach, and he didn't have patience for players who were a work in progress. I was learning the playbook as fast as I could and getting help from my teammates, but at times, it seemed like I was reading Hebrew. A few times, I was in the lineup during practice, didn't know the play, and would run the wrong route. Coach Sanford didn't take to that very well, and his frustration was obvious. I always had the mindset, if I wanted to be good at anything in life, I would have to keep practicing and keep studying until I got it right. That was no different with football! Whenever we weren't practicing or watching film, I was studying my playbook and asking my teammates for help.

My first game was scheduled for August 7, 1999, against the Denver Broncos, in Australia. I was nervous but eager to make this trip. During practice, I ran a deep route right down the sideline when one of the defensive backs hit my knee, and I felt a sharp pain radiate through my leg. I lie there thinking, "Are you kidding me? I ran this route many times during practice just fine, but this one time I landed wrong, and now I'm lying on the ground looking at my chances of making the fifty-three-man roster going up in smoke!" The trainers came over, and I told them I could hardly move my knee. They brought the golf cart, and my teammates took a knee in silence. The trainers didn't know whether I tore my medial collateral ligament, posterior cruciate ligament or my anterior cruciate ligament, until the x-rays revealed more about the injury. I couldn't make the trip to Australia to play Denver because I had to stay behind and recover. I went through an intense rehab, and I was back on the field to play against the San Francisco 49ers.

We took a charter flight to our hotel in San Francisco, and when we arrived at our hotel, there was a banquet table with all the food you could possibly eat. I had a quick bite with the rest of my teammates, and then we took a charter bus to Candlestick Park to get ready for the pregame. When I arrived at the stadium and walked to the locker room, my stomach was aching because I ate too much food, and all I could picture was seeing myself on the field taking my first NFL hit, catching my first pass, and making my first NFL touchdown.

I got suited up with all my gear, and then Coach Mike told all receivers to be on the field in five minutes. All the wide receivers and I walked out to the field, and my eyes lit up like fireworks. I couldn't believe I was about to play my first pregame in the NFL. All the quarterbacks came out the same time we did, and Jim Harbaugh, Erik Kramer, and Craig Whelihan called all the receivers to do routes. I felt great doing my routes and catching the ball. I did one more slant route over the middle of the field, and Jim Harbaugh threw me the ball. I caught it and ran up field a little bit. At the same moment, the legendary Jerry Rice caught a pass from Steve Young. We made eye contact and almost collided, as we slowed down not to interfere with each other's pregame. I looked at him and nodded my head to say *hello*, and he did the same. I went back to my side of the team and couldn't believe I was on the same field as Jerry Rice. I grew up watching him play, and now I was playing against him. It was a surreal moment I will never forget.

After pregame was over, the entire team went back to the locker room, and we all gathered around while our head coach, Mike Riley, gave his talk to us before we went on the field to play a hard sixty minutes of football. The chaplain prayed for us, as we knelt, and then it was time for battle. We all walked out holding hands, and it was as if someone turned up the volume full blast as thousands of fans for the Chargers and the 49ers were screaming like crazy. Junior Seau was on hype mode, as always. I stood on the sidelines, wondering when I would get the opportunity to go in and get some action. I was still learning the playbook, but I knew the only way to get better was to get experience playing in a live game. From the sidelines, I watched Robert Reed and Sirr Parker, rookies like myself, get in for some playing time. I patiently waited for my name to be called, but as the game progressed, Coach Sanford, who was my receiver coach, and our offensive coordinator, Geep, never called my name. I was furious standing on the sideline because I knew if I didn't get a chance to play, I couldn't showcase my skill to the coaches and prove that I was worth keeping on the fifty-three-man roster or the practice squad.

The game clock ticked down, and I didn't get in on my first NFL game. I felt the offensive coordinator didn't believe in me. My fate was sealed. According to him and my receiving coach, I wasn't NFL material. I called my agent and told Doc I wanted to play defense, like we originally agreed with Bobby, so I could do what I was good at. I said, "I know I have good hands, and the Chargers wanted to try me out as a wide receiver, but I could be more effective as a defensive back or free safety."

We arrived back in San Diego late that evening, and my wife picked me up at the San Diego Airport. I wasn't feeling good at all. I felt embarrassed because I told my family and friends to watch the game—but then, I didn't get in. The following week I was interviewed by the *San Diego Union Tribune,* and they asked me how I was feeling about camp. I expressed I was unhappy with the Chargers' organization for not allowing me to play defense. I explained that Bobby Beathard agreed to try me out as a wide receiver, and if things didn't work out, they would switch me to defensive back or free safety, in the middle of training camp. I had said too much.

After that article was published, things started to go downhill for me in the Chargers' organization. We were getting to the end of training camp, and the roster was getting trimmed down every week. As I was going to practice one day, I saw Sirr Parker with all his belongings—he had just been cut. I walked up to him and asked if he was okay. He said he wasn't because it was his dream to play football in the NFL, and now, he was in jeopardy of not being able to take care of his little girl. I felt badly, considering all during camp he was playing wide receiver when he was really a running back. More athletes were getting cut all the time. The following week, we had to play the Miami Dolphins at home but would scrimmage them first at our training camp facility. One of my good friends, Derrick, who played with me at Riverside Community College, was playing for Miami. It was going to be nice to see him. Miami brought all their boys to scrimmage us at UCSD, and it was a great prelude to what would happen in Sunday's game. There was much talk among the Miami players about my speed. They wanted to light me up badly. During scrimmage, the Miami Dolphins and my team got into a scuffle because one of their players was using slurs against one of our players. We didn't tolerate that from any team who were visitors at our practice facility.

Sunday's game couldn't come fast enough. It was a luxury playing at home because we didn't have to fly anywhere, and the Qualcomm Stadium was just minutes away from my house. I told everyone I knew to come see me play at Qualcomm, and I was confident, this time, I would get some playing time. We did our pregame warmup, and before I knew it, the referee was blowing the whistle for the captains to meet in the middle of the field for the coin toss. I was nervous because I could see myself running on the field for special teams and offense. I could hear the Miami Dolphins yelling my number because they wanted to see how fast I was on the football field. Unfortunately, that didn't happen. I waited the whole game on the sideline, and my number or name was never called. I remember Junior Seau was so mad I wasn't playing that he yelled at the coaches, "You have the fastest man in the NFL, but he's on the sideline not playing!" I was heartbroken. It seemed that absolutely none of the coaches wanted to give me a chance to showcase my football skills. The game was over, and I had to swallow another bitter pill of frustration because I didn't play. It seemed my time was running out because if I weren't playing, it was unlikely I would have a chance to make the team.

Right before our next game against the Denver Broncos, I walked into the locker room after practice, and there was a yellow card on my locker, asking me to go see the coach. I knew what it was about. I walked into Coach Mike's office, and he told me to have a seat. He said I had a lot of talent and was progressing learning the plays, but my injuries had set me back. He said they could only keep enough for the fifty-three-man roster, and the coaches had already picked their practice squad. As he was talking, I thought back to the time Bobby Beathard told my agent, Doc, if I didn't make the fifty-three-man roster that I would, at least, be on the practice squad. That didn't happen. Coach Riley also said to me I would be okay because I still had my contract with Reebok, which was true. But, I wanted to play in the NFL, and I knew in my heart I was as good as any player in the NFL.

I shook Coach Riley's hand and thanked him and the Chargers' organization for the opportunity. But, deep down inside, I was angry, sad, confused, and disappointed I didn't get the chance to show them what I could do on the football field. Throughout my life, I have experienced many setbacks which brought me to my knees, but I always got back up, regained my strength, and channeled all that negative energy into something positive. Now, that I was a free agent, all thirty-two teams in the National Football League were able to sign me, and hopefully, I could make someone's fifty-three-man roster, so I could get some playing time.

I called my wife, Chara, and told her my days with the Chargers were done. She was heartbroken because she knew my dream was to play in the NFL—not just on the sidelines but to be a dominant player on the field. I cried over the phone and shared with her I was sorry for letting her down. We also had to deal with the fact, we sold our new home in Riverside because Doc told me I would at least make the practice squad, so naturally, it made since to live in San Diego. I was only twenty-two at the time, and my wife was twenty. We were still newlyweds trying to figure out life.

I went back to Carmel Mountain in San Diego where my wife and I were staying. I had to make sure I was keeping fit, so I had a membership at a small gym called Frogs, about ten minutes from my house. Chara and I were going through some trying times as newlyweds. I was upset about my mother-in-law trying to run my household, my sister was in prison, I had anger issues, and I struggled with womanizing. For a year, I also kept having this same dream that I was running, and someone with a gun was chasing me. They would get close to me and shoot me in the back. My body would get warm in my dream, and I started shaking in my sleep. I thought it was a sign I was going to die. So, I wanted to get baptized immediately, but I didn't have a church home.

One day, I was at Frogs Gym lifting weights, and two gentlemen started talking about God. I chimed in and said I wanted to get baptized. One of the gentlemen looked at me and said, "This must be a sign from God because I'm a pastor." The gentleman's name was Jim Fulcher. I explained to him I wanted to get baptized because I was going to die. I asked him if he would baptize me right then. He said it didn't work that way, but we should set up a time to study the Bible. I said, "Sure!" I went back home after my workout and shared with my wife that I met a pastor in the gym by the name of Jim Fulcher. I told Chara he was going to come and study the Bible with me, and then when I was done, I would get baptized.

The following day Jim and another church member, Winslow Garnier, showed up at our apartment in Carmel Mountain. I introduced them to my wife, and Jim explained, before I could get baptized, he wanted me to understand why Jesus Christ died on the cross for my sins. Chara was skeptical at first, but she was desperate for a change. We were only two years into our marriage and were already having so many issues. We pulled out our Bibles and went through the scriptures. We discussed "sin" in Galatians 5:19, "love" in 1 Corinthians 13:4, faith, etc. I saw that I was so detached from living a godly life and was so disrespectful to my wife. Chara began to see my studying the Bible was a great thing and wanted to be on the same page and get her life together, too. Jim and Winslow connected her with Lynn, Jim's wife, and Ramona, who was Winslow's wife. Chara and I studied the Bible and prayed diligently, but as we were getting ready to fully dedicate our lives to God and stop living for the world, a phone call came.

Doc called and said the Raiders were going to sign me. I had already worked out for the Oakland Raiders months prior, and the coaches were excited about me. I told Doc I needed some time to think about it and discuss it with my wife. He said Oakland wouldn't wait around long, so I needed to make a decision fast. I shared the news with Chara, and she asked, "Why don't we get advice from Jim and Winslow?" So, we did. Jim said if I went to Oakland now, he didn't know if I would continue my studies from afar, and the progress we were making to strengthen our marriage would be in jeopardy. Chara and I were on pins and needles, so I made the decision to stay in San Diego and finish my studies to get baptized.

When Doc called back, I told him my dream was to play in the NFL, but my marriage and family had to come first. We needed to get our lives right with God. I told Doc that maybe after I'm done getting my family right with God, I could sign with another NFL team if it was too late with the Raiders. Doc was furious. He said he stuck his neck out to get me to sign with another NFL team, and I needed to be on the plane the next morning for Oakland. I felt so torn. I kept thinking; I didn't have to go through another training camp. I would be on the team, play the position I wanted to play, and have an opportunity to fight for a starting position. Then, I thought about my wife who I loved with all my heart. I knew football could be gone tomorrow, and most importantly, my salvation was at stake. I had been having a dream for a year that I was going to die, and quite frankly, I didn't want to go to hell, so I told Doc my decision was made. We hung up, and that was it. My chance to play in my first NFL game and be on the roster was gone like mist.

Chara and I completed our studies. I was baptized at Winslow's and Ramona's house in Poway, CA, and Chara was baptized shortly after. When I was dipped under water and came up, I was a brand-new man with a new soul. That dream I had of getting shot in the back faded away from my thoughts. For the first time in my life, I was at peace with myself, and my marriage was doing great!

Chapter 12

Broken

2000 was the year of the Olympics, and my eyes were fixed on winning the 400 meters at the Olympic Trials in Sacramento, CA. I was having a knock-out season—winning most of my races in the US. Prior to the Olympic Trials, I competed at the Steve Prefontaine Track and Field Classic in Eugene, OR and ran 44.7 seconds in the 400m, which was one of the fastest times in the world leading up to the Olympic Trials. My wife, at the time, Chara, was so excited about the great time I ran. She said, "The only person who is faster than you is Michael Johnson." She was right! I was on top of the world where I belonged, and I knew only sickness or injury could prevent me from getting on the Olympic podium. The world had already predicted that Michael would be Olympic champion in the 400 meters, but my goal was to spoil that narrative and bring the Olympic gold back to California.

I always appreciated Chara being with me because she was very supportive. She made sure I had all my business affairs in order before I stepped on the track to compete, which gave me peace of mind. When our time was up in Eugene, OR, we took a shuttle to the airport to head back home. On the plane, we were so happy about our trip! We cuddled and visualized ourselves at the Olympics in Sydney, Australia—basking in the joy of the dream as I received the Olympic gold medal.

We arrived safely to Ontario airport in California, grabbed our car, and drove an hour back to our home in Moreno Valley, CA. I pulled up in our driveway and told Chara, "Why don't you go open the door to the house, so we can get everything unpacked, shower, and go to bed." She got out of our SUV, walked up to the door to unlock it, and as soon as she put the key in the lock, I heard the house phone ring. Chara rushed to unlock the door. I'm still grabbing luggage, wondering who's calling, and how they knew we were home. I hear Chara screaming and crying, and I run inside to ask her what's wrong. With a river of tears running down her face, she said, "Your aunt Betty's on the phone and said your sister and her boyfriend killed your niece." I grabbed the phone from Chara and asked my aunt, "How is this possible?" She said my sister, Rosalyn, and her boyfriend suffocated, beat, and strangled my niece, Anjulette, to death. My heart was racing a mile a minute, and I could feel my blood heating up.

I stood there holding the phone in my hand in complete shock, and all I was thinking, at the time, was instead of one body bag, I wanted three. I was livid. Aunt Betty quickly dashed my dreams and said, they were in custody. They were quickly arrested and booked for murder. My thoughts were spinning. Pain and grief took over my body. All I could think about was the last time I spent with my niece.

I knew something was wrong, but I couldn't pinpoint it. I asked my sister and her boyfriend, "What's wrong with Anjulette?" They said she had mental problems and wasn't a good baby. Anjulette laid in her crib looking sad, lonely, and weak—while her twin sister was happy-go-lucky and thriving. I asked my sister if I could pick Anjulette up, and she said, "Yes." As I held her in my arms and comforted her, she felt so frail, her hair was thinning, and she seemed to have no joy inside her. I whispered to Chara and said, "Something isn't right here. We need to take Anjulette and get her out of here." Chara agreed something was wrong, but she said, "If you take her without the consent of Rosalyn and her boyfriend, you will go to jail for kidnapping." I was willing to take that risk, but I thought about how it would look in the public eye, so I opted to leave Anjulette in the house with her parents. Chara and I figured, if we called Child Protective Services on my sister and her boyfriend, maybe they would do a house check and take Anjulette away. Then, she could be with me or other family members. We called CPS, and they informed us a child welfare check was scheduled to ensure that Anjulette and her twin sister were ok. I felt a little more at ease, and I tried to focus my efforts on winning at the Olympic Trials in Sacramento.

I was scheduled to run in the first round of the 400m on July 14, 2000 and was confident I would breeze through the quarterfinals, semi-finals, and finals. Unfortunately, a week before the Olympic Trials, I developed a respiratory infection which sent me to see my asthma specialist. He prescribed prednisone during the week of the Olympic Trials to help decrease the inflammation in my lungs, so I could get more air flow to breathe. While I was on the track the day of the quarterfinals, I felt great during my warmup. I knew since Alvin Harrison, Derek Mills, and some up-and-coming 400m runners were in my heat, I was going to really have to work my first 300m, but after that, I could coast the last 100m. I walked to my lane, set the blocks, and did a couple of fifty-meter sprints. The starter blew the whistle for the runners to prepare for the start. I took my shirt and tights off, my heart was racing, and I was visualizing every phase of the race. The starter said, "Runners, take your mark." I squatted down in the blocks, ready to blast out like a rocket going into space. The starter says, "Set...." The stadium goes quiet, and you could have heard a pin drop in the stadium.

I'm in the blocks, looking straight ahead, and then the gun went off. I felt great ripping up my first hundred meters. I got on the backstretch, and I dropped my arms and let my legs do the work—and then I was coming into the second bend. My legs became weak, my arms felt like I had wrist weights on them, and I found myself fighting for dear life to qualify for the second round. Then, I saw Alvin pass me, then Derek, then another. I struggled to reach the finish line. I stood still for a minute like a "deer in headlights," wondering what in the heck just happened. I just ran a 44 less than three weeks ago, and now I was struggling to run a 46. I walked back to the tent, and a reporter asked me, "Ty, do you think you made it to the next round?" I said, "No! I could run 46 seconds in the 400m in my sleep, but today it was the real thing, and I looked like a kid in a high school meet trying to qualify for the league championships."

Chara was right there to comfort me, along with Coach Blackman, but I felt like a loser. I let everyone down—family, friends, my wife, my coach, and my shoe sponsor, Reebok, because I didn't make the Olympic team. Coach Blackman encouraged me and told me, perhaps if I could show my US National Team Coaches that I could run fast in the 400m, they would put me on the 4X400m relay because I did run 44 seconds twice in the 400m that year. Due to the stress from losing my niece, which led to my respiratory infection that required medication, I became sluggish—to the point where I had no life in my body.

I walked out of the Sacramento stadium defeated and depressed. I sat on the side of the curb outside the stadium and cried like a newborn baby, while the other runners prepared for their next heat. My time was up at the Olympic Trials. I only had one event, and one goal, and that was to make the Olympic team, but for whatever reason, it wasn't in the cards for me. I had been on top of the world and had my whole season planned—making the Olympic team, going to run on the European circuit, and then ultimately, becoming an Olympic champion.

I have always believed if something isn't broken, don't change it, but I went against my own advice. After the Olympic Trials' disappointment, I trained with Coach Blackman in the fall of 2000, and my training was superb. But, then, we had a difference of opinion, so I went to work with the Hall of Fame coach, Jim Bush, at UCLA, in the winter of 2001. I was in great shape from my fall training, and Coach Bush helped me get stronger. When it was time to compete in the spring of 2001, I won every race I entered. I, eventually, ran a personal best of 44.28 at the Occidental College Invitational. Coach Bush was happy, but he also chewed me out in front of everyone because I didn't run the race right. He was big on executing *your* race and not running someone else's race. I couldn't say anything back to him. I had to take it. I knew, even though I ran a personal best, I ran the race wrong, and I should have run an even better time in the 400m.

Other than my lack of execution at the Occidental meet, I was primed and ready to win the 400m at the Outdoor Nationals in June of 2001. Unfortunately, another setback happened prior to the Outdoor Nationals. This time I didn't get a respiratory infection, but weeks before the trials, I strained my hamstring. Chara and I couldn't believe, after all the hard work and sacrifice, another unfortunate circumstance happened. We arrived in Eugene, Oregon, for the Outdoor National Championships. Mentally, I was frustrated, but I wasn't going down without a fight. The day of the quarterfinals, I barely made it through to the semi-finals. The following round, I was out. I had the fastest time in the world, and once again, my season was over. I didn't make the world champion team, and I wasn't going to be a world champion in the 400m. I stood in shock and wondered how this could happen again. Was God trying to teach me a lesson? My thoughts were spinning out of control, and the pain and disappointment came over me like a plague. Chara was devastated too, because she had been so confident that this was my year—especially after what happened at the Olympic Trials the year before. Once again, reporters asked me about my plans for the future, and I told them my career in track and field was probably over.

I didn't go to Europe to run on the circuit. I went back to California broken, lost, angry, and disappointed that I let everyone down again. I couldn't shake the thought of my niece's tragic death, and it seemed no matter what I did or where I went, the pain of that traumatic event was destroying me day by day. I didn't compete for the rest of the year, but I did decide to go back and finish my AA degree at San Bernardino Valley College. I had to take eighteen units to get my degree by December, and that's what I did.

I applied to become a group counselor for the Riverside Probation Department in Riverside. I passed my online test, background check, and psychological evaluation and was hired in March of 2002. Running track again was the last thing on my mind. My focus was taking care of my family, providing support to my family during my sister's murder trial, and being there for my son. I was, eventually, subpoenaed by the Riverside District Attorney to give my account of my sister's mental state. I told the DA she never drank alcohol or did drugs, but she was lazy and made bad choices. I explained to the DA that her boyfriend was bad business, and he had no ambition to work or make good decisions. The DA asked me if I believed my sister was capable of murder, and I said, "Yes." I was very angry and wanted revenge for what she did to my niece. I wanted her and her boyfriend to get the death penalty for taking an innocent life.

I was doing great at my new job as a group counselor, but the burden of my sister's murder trial was taking its toll on me. On June 10, 2002, two years to the day after my sister murdered my niece, I finally hit my breaking point. I was at home in Moreno Valley, CA, and my thoughts were very erratic. I was arguing with Chara about my sister, and I kept thinking, "Why didn't I prevent Rosalyn and her boyfriend from murdering my niece?" I thought I was God, and I thought I should have protected my niece. I kept thinking, "Why did you choose your career over your niece? You should have taken her and risked going to jail to save her life."

I walked into my garage and found a rope that was lying on a cardboard box. I never knew how to tie a noose, but that day I became an expert. I grabbed a chair and wrapped the rope around a solid beam of wood in my garage. I had to make sure the height was good because I didn't want my feet to touch the ground. I secured everything, so the rope wouldn't break. I stepped up on the chair, took the noose, and wrapped it around my neck. Then, Chara walked into the garage, started screaming and crying, telling me not to kill myself. I yelled at her, "I don't care what happens to me! I shouldn't have let my niece die!" She yelled at me, "It wasn't your fault! You're not God! You couldn't have known your sister and her boyfriend were going to kill your niece!"

I stood on the chair, and I felt a sense of peace that it was time for me to die. I started to justify to myself that I had lived a good life. After all, I won medals on the world stage and made it out of the ghetto. Now, it was time to meet my maker. Satan wanted my soul, and he wanted it badly. In my eyes, hope was non-existent, and the only way out of my pain and suffering was death. Chara grabbed her phone and called 911. She told the 911 operator I was going to hang myself. The 911 operator was trying to have her get me down from the chair, but I was yelling, "I'm going to kill myself!" This went on for about five minutes, which really seemed like fifty minutes.

Seeing Chara crying and begging me to come down, I started to think about my son Malik. My father wasn't in my life, and if I were to take my life, Malik would not have a father. I thought, even though Chara and I had had our difficult days, I loved her very much, and I didn't want to leave her. In the midst of my pain, I thought about God, and despite all the tragedy I'd been through, God could heal anybody, including me.

I stepped down from the chair with tears running down my face. By then, the cops were at the door. The officers asked me if I tried to hang myself, and I said, "Yes, but I will be okay." They informed me that because a call came in for a suicide, they would have to handcuff me for their safety and mine, and I would need to go to a mental hospital for a seventy-two-hour evaluation. I was like, "You're not taking me anywhere." Chara was screaming and crying, telling me, "Ty, let them take you!" The officers told me they wouldn't hurt me but just wanted to help me. I was going to put up a fight before I let them take me, but once again, I looked at Chara. Seeing the tears roll down her face broke me at that moment, and I gave up. The officers handcuffed me and put me in the back of the police car. I was taken to the mental hospital for evaluation.

When I arrived at the mental hospital in handcuffs, I was taken to a white room and instructed to sit.. The officer who handcuffed me, asked me, "If we take the handcuffs off, you're not going to hurt yourself?" I replied, "No." At this time, I was an employee of the Riverside Probation Department, and my job was minutes from the mental hospital. I felt embarrassed while I was in there because I thought," "What if my boss and co-workers find out what I did? They may fire me or think I was crazy." I just had a mental breakdown from all the pain and suffering in my life that created a dark storm with me trying to kill myself. The doctor came in to evaluate me after I had an hour to calm down and grapple with the reality that I almost took my own life. The doctor asked me if I would try and kill myself again, and I said, "No." He asked me if I still felt depressed, and I said, "No." I told him I was at a low point in my life. I told him who I was and about my career as a track and field athlete. He was impressed and shortly after my evaluation, he said I was free to go home—only into the care of my wife.

When I called Chara and told her the doctor was letting me go, she couldn't believe it. She said you were supposed to be held for seventy-two hours. I said, "I know, but they let me go." When Chara arrived, signed me out, and I got in the car, she asked me how I felt. I said I still felt depressed. She asked, "Why didn't you tell the doctor that?" I replied, "I didn't want to stay in there with all those crazy people, so I told them what they wanted to hear." Chara wasn't happy at all with what I said, and she told me she didn't want to ever go through that experience again. We drove home, and all I could think about were the events which led up to this traumatic moment in my life.

Suicide attempts can happen at any moment to anyone. It doesn't matter what color you are, how rich you are, your status, or how good you look. If you don't open up with all the hurt and pain you're going through in your life, you will lose hope, and all the bad will put you in a very vulnerable place, causing you to want to end your life. If that's you, I encourage you to call the suicide hotline if you are considering taking your own life, or if you know of someone who wants to take their life: 1-800-273-8255.

Chapter 13

The Cost of Being Clean

Let's go back to the day of my race at the 2003 World Championships in France. The memory of that day replays in my mind all the time. I felt like I was walking onto a battlefield to take aim at my competitors but also my own demons. My heart was pounding in my chest as if this were the fight of my life. I knew I had to run two times before I reached the finals, and my first test would be to run the prelims, second the semi-finals, and third the finals. The sound from the crowd was deafening during the prelims, but now, as I lined up for the final, it seemed eerily quiet. I wondered if the runners in the lanes next to me had trained as hard as I had. But, I didn't care. I felt like a predator, ready to devour my competition.

I ran the 400m semi-final in 44.60 seconds with ease. I figured if I ran that well in the semi-finals, in the finals I could do 44 flat or even 43.8 and win it all. I got out my first one-hundred meters, coasted into the backstretch and was eating up the field. I kicked at 180 meters and was feeling great until the final 150 meters. That's when Jerome Young and Calvin Harrison came storming around the bend. My body started to lock up, and I started to panic. I kept telling myself, "Ty, relax, maintain your mechanics." My body went into shock, my form broke down, and the tank went empty. I finished second to Jerome Young. My perfect season was over. I was not the world champion. I stood on the track looking at the huge screen in disbelief.

As the reality of coming in second sunk in, I managed to gather myself and make it over to the awards stand. Jerome Young was one of my best friends, my roommate on the road, and someone I shared so much with. He won. He was the better runner that day. He was the world champion. I was second. We received our medals, and I went to shake his hand and congratulate him. He took my hand but looked away. He wouldn't look me in the eye.

It would take five more years for me to learn the reason why. He was doping. He tested positive for performance-enhancing drugs (PEDs) in 2004, in France, and admitted he had been using them since before the 2003 Worlds. I felt robbed of my rightful title. I was upgraded to world champion in 2009 by the International Association of Athletics Federation (IAAF), now known as World Athletics, but I wanted more than that. I reached out to my national governing body, USA Track & Field (USATF), asking them to let the IAAF know I wanted to receive my world championship medal at the 2009 World Outdoor Championships in Berlin. My request was denied. Essentially, I was told by Nick Davies, an IAAF spokesperson, that the IAAF preferred to promote the success of a clean athlete in his own country rather than to promote the consequences of doping on a world stage in front of billions of TV viewers. This left me frustrated and furious that the IAAF could deny me the right to share my moment with the world. I was a clean athlete and would never jeopardize my integrity or that of my family, fans, and my US Federation. Later, I learned our team was disqualified as world champions in the 4X400m relay, also in 2003, since Jerome Young was on that team. I couldn't believe it.

Ultimately, I had to settle for getting my world championship medal at the US Outdoor National Championships in Eugene, Oregon. The IAAF no longer recognized Jerome Young as the world champion, and because of that, he wasn't compensated. The compounding impact on my life from this doping scandal was significant. And, I didn't fully realize then what being a clean athlete would cost me.

I lost five years of benefitting financially from being a world champion. I ended up losing three world championship gold medals in relays and a world record because my teammates were doping. Being upgraded to world champion in 2009—a full six years after the Balco scandal—I was deprived of the ESPYS, the Jesse Owens awards, and many other honors and recognitions. Drugs took my teammates and because I refused to take them, drugs took me. Nobody wanted to be around a clean athlete. Nobody was interested in what I was saying. To them, I was an outsider, and then I became a pariah the entire sport was afraid of—including sponsors. It appeared that believing in what was right and good meant nothing. The truth is supposed to set you free but depending on who you're dealing with, it can get you blackballed.

There is lots of money to be made running races. Losing three world championship gold medals, a world record, and a world championship title cost me millions in sponsorship and prize money—not to mention endorsements and interest I would have made on that prize money—all because others chose to dope.

Throughout my eleven-year track and field career, I've seen many athletes who were caught doping, the consequences, and even temporary rewards that come with it. I've seen athletes win medals at the world or Olympic level, but when they were caught doping, they'd take advantage of the platform and go make more money by appearing on TV, making documentaries, and writing books to deny the guilt. I've seen athletes banned for a period of time, banned for life, and even commit suicide. When an athlete cheats, they not only cheat themselves, but their fans, sponsors, federation, family members, and teammates. For athletes like myself who competed clean, we don't have the luxury of going back in time to stand on a podium and receive our medals in front of the world. We can't recover our prize.

What always amazed me throughout my career is, while I was getting ready for an event, I'd see needles in the bathroom from athletes doping right before a race. I knew if I wanted to be dominant and put fear in athletes who were doping, I would have to beat them while they were taking performance-enhancing drugs. I *did* that for many years—beating my competitors who were doping. I watched them, one by one, get caught doping or retire out of frustration because they were only as good as the drugs they were taking.

I've spent my whole life beating the odds and turning a bad situation into something good. Because of the doping scandals and setbacks, I started educating student athletes and using my platform to educate athletes about doping. I trained athletes to compete clean. Now, I am expanding my reach with my platform to include both athletes and non-athletes. I am completely aware that fighting doping and recreational drugs is an ongoing battle, but if I can educate and share my story to the youth, and save one, five, or ten of them from making a bad choice, then I've done my job.

These are the medals I lost due to my teammates doping admissions:

1. 4X400m relay 1997 World Outdoor Championships — Gold (Athens, Greece)
2. 4X400m relay 1998 Goodwill Games- world record and Gold medal (Uniondale, New York)
3. 4X400m relay 2003 World Indoor Championships- Gold (Birmingham, England)
4. 4x400m relay 2003 World Outdoor Championships- Gold (Saint Denis, France)

Chapter 14

Redemption

Before the start of my fall program to prepare for the 1998 track and field season, Coach Blackman and I had a meeting to go over my goals, my weight room, practice and competition schedule to make sure we were both on the same page. I aimed to be the number one 400m runner in the world. My fall training went as planned, and I was in extraordinarily strong shape for the season. Coach Blackman and I had some differences of opinion about training, so my agent, Roger Lipkis, and Pete Peterson asked Hall of Fame Coach, Jim Bush, if he would be interested in training me, and he agreed. Jim Bush trained some great 400m runners who weren't fast when he first worked with them, but after a year or two with him, they were winning NCAA, Olympic, and world titles.

After I won the bronze medal at the 1997 World Outdoor Championships in Athens, Greece, TBS decided to interview me and air my interview during the week of the Goodwill Games. The interview segment profiled my life, and I was excited to share some of my story with the world. I ran a variety of meets on the international circuit, and when it was time to travel to Uniondale, New York, for the Goodwill Games, I was primed and ready.

Chara traveled with me to the Goodwill Games. She really helped me stay focused, made sure I had all my equipment, and kept my appointments. My first event was the 200m, and I came in second behind Ato Bolden. I, sincerely, thought I was going to win the 200m, but I was charged with a false start. I waited in the blocks longer to make sure I didn't get another false start, because if I did, I'd be eliminated from the race. This caused me to get a slower start, and running against pure sprinters like Ato Bolden, you had to get out quickly. I laughed and was already thinking of the 400m because it was going to be a real battle between me and Michael Johnson. I was projected to be runner-up to Michael, and that didn't sit well with me.

The day before my race, I made sure I ate well, rested, took an ice bath, and got a massage. When it was time for the 400m, all eyes were on me and Michael, and the showdown was being built up on TV and newspapers for fans and athletes. I strolled on the track, rocking my headband, while Chara watched me from the stands. I said my prayer, visualized my race, and before I knew it, the gun went off, and all the 400m runners were blazing around the first 100m on the track. I ran a very conservative race my first 200m, which wasn't good because Michael hit the 200m and was accelerating to take command. I tried to catch him, but it was too late. I had won another silver medal. I made the same costly mistake I had made at the World Championships in Athens—waiting too long to kick. I wasn't pleased with my performance because I hate to lose, but I tried to learn a lesson from it.

I had one more event—the 4X400m relay. I would be joined by Michael, Jerome Young, and Antonio Pettigrew. Our goal for team USA was to win another gold medal for our country. With the team we had, it was sure to be a slam dunk. I was set to run third leg, and Michael was going to run anchor. We didn't practice together as a team because all of us were veterans and knew how to run the 400m relay. The key was to make sure we each got a good takeoff to receive the baton in the zone and to make sure we had a good exchange with the person receiving the baton. The 4X400m relay would close out the Goodwill Games for the track and field portion, and the entire world wanted to see how fast our relay team would run. Before we stepped on the track, I was warming up, and a freak accident almost happened. A stadium groundskeeper was driving a golf cart, and as I was doing some sprints on the grass, he rode across my path and almost hit me. I may not have been friends with a large number of athletes on the warm-up track from my country or from other countries, but this guy almost got mobbed by athletes from all over the world. Thank God for my quick reaction to move out of the way, because if I hadn't, he would have run me over and possibly broken my legs.

I shrugged it off quickly and focused on the job that was in front of me. We stepped on the track, and Jerome ran a fast first leg, and I was like, "Whoa!" Because, when I looked at the clock, it said 43, but it was officially 44. Then, Antonio ran a 43. I ran a 43, and Michael also ran a 43. We broke the world record for the 4x400m relay. The crowd went nuts! Chara was so excited that she was crying. It was a memorable night that remains with me today. I believe if it hadn't been for God's blessings, having Coach Blackman and Coach Jim Bush laying out the blueprint for my track season, and making sure my fall training was rock solid, I wouldn't have walked away with two silver medals, a gold medal, at the Goodwill games, and a world record.

I finished off the rest of my season running overseas. Then, I came home to prepare to marry Chara at Riverside Baptist Church on September 26, 1998. My best friend, Mike, gave me a bachelor party the day before the wedding that didn't end well. Mike and I got crazy drunk and decided to take some girls, who came to entertain me, back home. I was in the back seat talking to one of the girls, and all of a sudden, I passed out. When I woke up, there were five police cars surrounding my brand-new Mitsubishi Eclipse. As I woke up to the bright lights and opened the door, the officer asked me if I was alright. I said, "Yes." He told me he was getting ready to call the paramedics because they had been banging on the window for ten minutes, thinking I might be dead. I asked the police officer about my friend Mike, and he said Mike was going to jail for driving under the influence. That sobered me up quickly! Mike was supposed to be my best man in my wedding the next day! What was I going to tell his mom, who is like my mom? I asked the officer if I could have my keys, and he said, "No." I kept asking. Then, he said, "I could tow your car and take you to jail, or you can walk home." I lived in Chino Hills at the time, which was an awfully long walk from where I was in Ontario. The officer told me to find a way home and said we were lucky to be alive because Mike had been swerving all over the freeway. I called and asked one of my friends to pick me up and take me home. I called

Mike's mom, Annette, and told her Mike was in jail. She was extremely upset with us for being irresponsible. We were *very* irresponsible, and we both could have died. Mike was able to get out of jail the next morning for my wedding. I was relieved.

Chara couldn't believe what a mess we had gotten ourselves into, but she was still ready to get married. After the wedding, we honeymooned in Jamaica for a week at an exclusive resort called Sandals. After our honeymoon, we bought a new home in Riverside and a brand-new car. We both were excited about our new home, which was in a quiet neighborhood. My son, Malik, had his own room, and we had a nice-sized backyard. I was a married man with a complete family now, and my next goal was to make it to the NFL.

I got tired of driving to UCLA and West LA College for track practice with Coach Bush. I asked Coach Blackman if we could reconcile, so he could train me again. He agreed, but we quickly hit a bump in the road and had more disagreements, so I was soon off working with Innocent, who was a great 400m runner from Nigeria. At the same time, this is when I hired Doc, an NFL agent, to help prep me for my NFL workouts.

As I said before, things didn't go as planned with the San Diego Chargers or the Oakland Raiders, so I refocused my efforts to solely running track to prepare for the 2000 Olympics. Everything seemed to be on the upswing until my niece was tragically killed. Then, the asthma attack which led to the medicine, dulled my efforts. When I was knocked out of the first round at the Olympic Trials in Sacramento, I couldn't function. I spent the summer depressed, with no desire to run again. My life seemed to be spinning out of control, and I didn't know who I was, or where I wanted to go. My sister's murder trial, family feuds, and my illness had all taken a toll on me—mentally and physically. I'd been fighting the good fight my whole life, and in 2006, I was having another great year in track and field when I made the 4X400m relay team for the Indoor World Championships in Moscow, Russia. This would be my second go round competing in Russia, and my main goal was to come away with another world championship gold medal, and I did. I felt my 2006 track and field season was going to be more successful than my 2005 season.

After the Indoor World Championships in Russia, I flew back home to prepare for my outdoor season. I also needed to send my passport to the United States Department State Passport Center to get more pages, so I could travel back to Europe to compete. A few weeks passed, and I received a letter from the US Passport Center, notifying me that my passport had been confiscated because I was in arrears for owing back child support in the amount of twenty-two thousand dollars. I knew that couldn't be right because I had an official child support order in which I agreed and was obligated to pay a certain amount to help take care of my son. I went into panic mode, called my agent in Atlanta, and told her what was going on. We decided to hire an attorney to get to the bottom of everything.

I hired an attorney in my hometown of Riverside, CA, and during my first appointment with her, she looked me directly in the eyes and asked me if I paid my child support. I told her emphatically, "Yes!" I gathered all the child support cashier's check receipts I kept from making my child support payments. She told me to be patient, and she would petition the US Passport Center and Courts to release my passport.

I continued my training, but I couldn't help to think, if I didn't get my passport back, I would not be able to honor my shoe contract and make money overseas to help financially support my family. My attorney called me one day and told me that if I made a payment to bring my balance below five thousand dollars, I would be able to get my passport back. I had competed in some track meets throughout the US, so I had earned more than enough to get my balance lower than five thousand. My agent wired me over seventeen thousand, and I paid the money directly to the child support division office in Riverside.

In the meantime, while I was trying to figure out my legal troubles, I was using the last of the money I had in my savings to pay for our mortgage, utility bills, gas, and car insurance, etc. Chara and I were becoming stressed. My attorney called and told me she received the info from the child support division that I made the payment, and my passport should soon be released. That didn't happen. My agent had track meets in Europe all lined up, and the meet promoters wanted to know when I'd arrive. I did my best to call my attorney every day to follow up, but everything was at a standstill, waiting for the US Passport Center to release my passport. Finally, my attorney called me to say my passport had been released, but the damage had already been done.

Our savings ran out, and our home was being foreclosed on. We sold our cars and downgraded to one vehicle, but none of that put a dent in the debt we owed. I told my attorney I was losing my home, and she said we needed to have a meeting with the District Attorney to try and figure out what was going on. I went with my attorney and met with the DA who asked me if I had proof I paid my child support. I showed her all the cashier's checks I had kept to help take care of my son. The DA was amazed I kept all my cashier's check receipts and told me they would calculate everything to see if I was owed back anything. I stood there in disbelief knowing that I had worked so hard to buy my home with my blood, sweat, and tears from competing all over the world in track and field. There were days when my asthma flared up, and I was in the hospital, but as soon as I was released, I was back training, working hard to earn enough money to buy a house for my wife and son.

In the end, I was losing my home because of mis-communication. My agent called again and asked if I had my passport because I was supposed to be in Europe within a couple of days. I told her I still did not have it. She told me if I did not go to Europe to compete, it wouldn't look good for my reputation, but there was nothing I could do. My wife, Chara, and I ran out of time. A letter came in the mail that said we would have three days to move as soon as the sheriff placed the foreclosure notice on our door. It seemed as if the time flew by, and the sheriff came to put a three-day notice to move out on our door. I rented a U-Haul and started loading our belongings, so we could put them in storage. My mother- in-law offered me and my wife to move in with her, but I didn't want to because I felt embarrassed that I ran out of money and was broke.

Months prior, I was on top of the world, winning another world championship gold medal, and now I was left with a truck filled with our belongings, no money, a career in jeopardy, and stress in my marriage. I packed everything within the three-day window, and Chara went to spend a couple of nights at her parent's house. I stayed in my home for one last night. I cried like a baby and drank like a sailor. I felt like a failure and was embarrassed I let myself and my family down. What drove the knife deeper into my heart was when I got a call from my attorney. She told me the DA finished up the calculations, and I had overpaid child support by more than eleven thousand dollars. I told my attorney I was happy to get a refund for the overpayment, but it was too late because my house was gone. She fought hard to get my passport back, but unfortunately, the time ran out on me. This whole ordeal left me depressed, angry, frustrated, and lonely. Shortly after, my marriage fell apart. Chara and I separated and eventually got divorced.

I attempted to make a comeback for the 2007 track and field season, but in March of 2007, I had to get a microdiscectomy for a bulging disc in my back, which was hitting my sciatic nerve. My surgeon told me days before the surgery, I was in good shape, and the surgery would only take about forty-five minutes. I was happy about that, considering I wanted to get back to training as soon as possible to prepare for the US Outdoor Nationals. The day of my surgery, I felt very uneasy about the procedure, so I asked to pray with a priest, and my request was granted. A priest came to the waiting area to pray with me while I waited for surgery, and I felt much better. The nurses came and prepped me for surgery. As I put on my gown and what looked like a shower cap on my head, the nurses had me get on a bed with wheels, to be pushed to the operating room. As I lie on the bed, looking up at the lights in the operating room, my surgeon tells me to count to ten. Before I knew it, I was out like a light.

When I woke up, I was in an Intensive Care Unit. I asked the doctor what happened, and he said I was under longer than expected, and because of the nature of my surgery, they were taking precautions to make sure I was going to be okay. I was hooked up to lots of monitors because I started having several complications with my health. I couldn't believe what was happening to me. Before surgery, I was fit and ready to compete, and now I was lying in a hospital bed in ICU. I had the sweetest nurses, and every day they encouraged me that I'd get better. I spent many days crying and wondering if one day, I would go to sleep and never wake up again. What consumed me a lot was thinking if I did pass away, I didn't want to die not having my loved ones with me.

During my time in ICU, my rehab consisted of walking from my bed to the door, which was about four feet away. When I got stronger, I would walk to the hallway and back, which was about ten or fifteen feet away. I stayed in ICU for four days, and then I went home. It was very humbling, walking around with a back brace, using a walker, and wearing long socks that helped prevent blood clots. I called Coach Blackman and told him I wanted to compete at the US Outdoor National Championships, and he was on board. Trying to make the team wasn't my priority because I knew my rehab would take a couple of months, and I would only have a month to get in some training and be race sharp.

My doctors, however, told me my track and field season was over for 2007, and I needed to use the year to recover. But, I wasn't trying to hear that. I was on the last year of my shoe contract, and I wanted to show my shoe company that, although I wasn't in world-class sprinter shape, I still could run with the best of them. I rehabbed for a couple of months, trained on the track and in the weight room for over a month, and then went to the US Outdoor National Championships in Indianapolis, Indiana.

I didn't perform well at the Outdoor National Championships as expected, but I did prove to my sponsor, despite being in ICU and with minimal training, I was honoring my contract. I went to Europe to run on the circuit, with the hope my shoe sponsor would re-sign me for one more year, so I could try to make the 2008 Olympic team. However, at the end of the season, my agent informed me my shoe sponsor wasn't going to renew my contract. I did the best I could to prepare for the 2008 Olympic Trials, but it was hard to train consistently when I no longer had a steady income from my shoe sponsor in order to eat properly, buy training equipment, and have a steady place to live.

I ran in a few track meets throughout California and was able to qualify for the Olympic Trials in Eugene, Oregon, by running a fast-enough time at the UCLA Track and Field Invitational. I arrived in Oregon and got settled in my hotel, so I could prepare to run the quarterfinals in the 400m in the upcoming days. I had little money, so I was rationing it to get through my time at the Olympic Trials.

The day of my race I felt okay, but I knew I wasn't in great shape. I went through my normal warm-up routine, and when it was time to report to the call room, so I could check in to get my bib number, I felt this overwhelming sense of peace. I walked out to the track on Hayward field, and the crowd was roaring like a lion. I took off my running tights, and I put on my headband to prepare for my last battle. In my mind, if I was leaving the sport for good, I was going out fighting. The starter blew the whistle for the runners to get in the blocks. I said my prayers; the starter gave the commands, and the gun went off. I blasted out like a rocket and was feeling fine until I hit about 150m to go, and my body said, "No, mas." I finished the race, and my career in track and field was over. I walked over to the tent where all the reporters were waiting to interview the athletes, and I told a long-time reporter who covered my career that I was retiring. He wished me the best of luck, and I spent my last days in Oregon watching a few races before I traveled back to Southern California.

I believe God's timing is always right on time. For over a year, I didn't have a vehicle, but God blessed me to receive a check from my sponsor for being upgraded to world champion in the 400m. I used some of the funds to buy a truck, and the rest I used to take care of my two kids, pay bills, and buy food. I was having an issue staying with family, so I became homeless and started living in my truck. I had been hopping around sleeping on friends' and families' sofas for about three months. My girlfriend, Monica, unexpectedly became pregnant, which made me realize I needed to get my life together, so I could help take care of her and my unborn child.

I got a job in Orange County, CA, working as a personal trainer. No one at my job knew I was homeless and living in my car because I would always have a smile on my face. I always talked to my co-workers and was energetic. I would work out early in the morning, shower after, and have a sandwich for breakfast. When my shift was over, I would be extremely tired from working all day, would drive my truck to a nearby apartment, and park outside as if I were one of the tenants. Everything I owned was in my truck. I would buy food that wouldn't spoil and keep it on one side of the truck and my clothes on the other side. Many nights, I would be so tired, I wouldn't lock my truck because I would pass out in the driver's seat. During the times it was cold, I didn't want to drive to a store and burn gas, so I would urinate in a bottle and throw it out in the morning.

I cried a lot while listening to slow songs on the radio and wondered why I was suffering like this. I questioned whether God loved me and whether He heard my prayers. I was in despair, but I knew deep down the only person who could help me overcome my hardship was God. One day after work, I decided to go see an old track friend, Brandy, who coached at Cal State Fullerton. She used to run track herself, and now she was the sprint coach, developing student athletes. We visited for a while, and later that day, I called her and shared with her my frustration that my life was not going the way I planned. She asked me where I was living, and I told her I was living in my truck. She told me I could come and sleep on her sofa, but I declined because I didn't want to burden her with my problems. She told me I wouldn't be a burden, and she didn't want to see me living in my truck. She knew I had a baby on the way with Monica and just wanted to help me because I was in a difficult place in my life. She gave me a key to her home and made me feel like family. Every day, she would encourage me that my life would get better. Monica delivered our baby girl in March of 2010, and we saved up enough money to rent an apartment in Murrieta, California.

I defied many odds to become a professional track and field athlete. God blessed me to win many world titles, and I got to travel the world and do something I loved to do. Today, my wife, Monica, and I have six children between the two of us, and we've traveled the country together, as she serves the country as an enlisted soldier. I wouldn't have asked for a different or a better path in life. Through the many ups and downs, the highs and lows, it was all for a greater purpose. As we close the last chapter on this book, I want to leave you with the life lessons which have carried me along my journey. My hope is that you turn every trauma you face in life into a triumph that will leave a lasting legacy, so that against all odds, you, too, can achieve greatness.

TYREE'S TOP TEN TAKEAWAYS FOR SUCCESS

1. Stop trying to be perfect—perfect doesn't exist. The goal is to work towards becoming better every day. Trying to be perfect will leave you angry, stressed, depressed, and frustrated.
2. If you see yourself where you want to be, then that's where you're going to be. We all want that specific job, relationship, car, etc. If you don't see yourself getting what you want, you will not have what you want.
3. Write down specific goals and put them where you can see them. Say them aloud every day to yourself, or someone you're close to. Statistically speaking, you're more likely to accomplish your goals when you write them on paper, post them where you can see them, and say them out loud to yourself.
4. What you think is what you will attract. If you think negative thoughts, watch negative things, listen to negative things, and spend time with negative people, you will attract negativity. Change your negative thinking, and you will see how much better your life will become.
5. When you're going through troubling times in your life, focus on gratitude. It will help you appreciate all the good things you have in your life instead of what you don't have. Make a list of all the good things you have in your life and put it up on your bedroom wall or on your refrigerator for daily encouragement.
6. Be what you want to be. If you're not what you want to be yet, start acting as if you *are* what you want to be. If your goal is to be

an entrepreneur, start acting like one now by getting your website, business cards, professional attire, etc.

7. Love who you are and not who someone else wants you to be. No one can make you happy—only you can make yourself happy. If you base your happiness on a person or a thing, once that person or thing is gone, your happiness is gone.

8. Who you hang around, will determine who you will become. Successful people hang around successful people, and unsuccessful people hang around with each other. Birds of a feather flock together.

9. Don't be afraid to lose. Many of us feel that when we lose in life, life is over. That's not true. Life is just beginning. Losing doesn't mean you're a loser; it just means you need more practice to get better, and you may eventually find something that aligns more with who you were meant to be. It's all a lesson.

10. Value who you are. Never devalue yourself because someone believes you are not worthy. You ARE worthy. Don't let anyone tell you otherwise.

About Tyree Washington

Tyree Washington is a 400m world champion in track and field, an NFL alumni, and a former law enforcement peace officer. Today, Tyree is a speaker, trainer, and coach who encourages, motivates, and inspires people from all walks of life. His message is regardless of the adversity you may encounter, if you act as if your situation has already changed, maintain a positive mindset, and surround yourself with positive people, there is no adversity you cannot overcome.

Visit: www.tyreeswashington.com to learn more about Tyree's events and speaking engagements.

Printed in the USA
CPSIA information can be obtained
at www.ICGtesting.com
LVHW041152171023
761328LV00061B/925